The Great Black North is a contemporary remix of the story of Black Canada. Told through the intertwining tapestry of poetic forms found on the page and stage, *The Great Black North* presents some missing pieces of the jigsaw puzzle that help fit together a poetic picture of the Black Canadian experience.

Many African Canadians know their history in North America since the 17th century. However, the rest of the world may be unaware of the history of enslaved Africans and slave auctions north of the 49th parallel, as well as the free Blacks, Loyalists and Maroons who made their journeys to the "promised land" of Canada. *The Great Black North* should be a valuable resource for the preservation of culture that is written and/or performed as dub poetry, spoken word and slam. At the heart of this book is a poetic blend of literary and oral traditions that recognizes the past and present as they form a tangible foundation for future generations of poets.

This collection of over 90 poets documents the many styles that Black Canadians use to express themselves. The rhythms felt in *The Great Black North* stem from the vibrant pulse of poets such as the much translated and internationally honoured Africadian George Elliott Clarke; Ian Keteku, who was crowned the 2010 World Poetry Slam champion; Lillian Allen, founder of the dub poetry tradition in Canada; and Afua Cooper, who brought to light the hanging of an enslaved African woman, Marie-Joseph Angélique, for the alleged burning of Montreal in 1734. Olive Senior, Frederick Ward, Lorna Goodison, Tanya Evanson, Pamela Mordecai, and Harold Head are just a few of the many other poets in the anthology who have pieced together this timely map of Black Canada.

Also by Valerie Mason-John:

Author

Making Black Waves,
co-authored with Ann Khambatta, 1993.

Borrowed Body, 2005.

Detox Your Heart, 2006.

Broken Voices – Untouchable Women Speak Out, 2008.

Editor

Black Art and Culture on the Mainland of Europe, 1992.

Talking Black: African and Asian Lesbians Speak Out, 1994.

Bleeding My Soul (poetry/prose anthology), 2006.

CDs

The Perfect Road, 2009.

Also by Kevan Anthony Cameron:

Chapbooks

P.an A.fricanism I.s D.ead, 2008.

Seventh Sense: Poems by Scruffmouth, 2009.

New Word Order, 2010.

*Elementality: Graphic Poetry From the Spoken Notebook of
Scruffmouth the Scribe,* 2011.

Black Ever Since, 2012.

CDs

Spoken Notebook, 2013.

The Great Black North

CONTEMPORARY AFRICAN CANADIAN POETRY

Selected and Edited by Valerie Mason-John
& Kevan Anthony Cameron

Preface by Karina Vernon

Introduction by George Elliott Clarke

 **Frontenac House Poetry**

Calgary, Alberta

Book design: Epix Design

Cover design: "Landscape", mixed media on canvas, 2012, by David Woods, Halifax, N.S. _david.woods@banns.ca_

"Temitope" by Pamela Mordecai, from the collection _Subversive Sonnets_ (2012), reprinted by permission of the poet and TSAR Publications.

"mAri Performs" was originally published in _She_ copyright © 2000 by Claire Harris. Reprinted by permission of Goose Lane Editions.

"Resume" by Harold Head from the anthology _Canada In Us Now,_ NC Press Ltd – 1976. By permission of the author.

Library and Archives Canada Cataloguing in Publication

The great Black North: contemporary African Canadian poetry / Valerie Mason-John & Kevan Anthony Cameron.

Also issued in electronic format.

ISBN 978-1-897181-83-6

1. Canadian poetry (English)--Black Canadian authors. 2. African Canadian poetry

(English)--21st century. I. Mason-John, Valerie, 1962- II. Cameron, Kevan Anthony, 1979-

PS8283.B55G74 2012 C811'.6080896071 C2012-906695-8

Frontenac House gratefully acknowledges the support of the Canada Council for the Arts for our publishing program. We also thank the Government of Alberta Multimedia Development Fund for their support of our publishing program.

Canada Council   Conseil des Arts
for the Arts   du Canada

**Government
of Alberta** ■

Printed and bound in Canada
Published by Frontenac House
1138 Frontenac Ave SW
Calgary, Alberta, T2T 1B6, Canada

Tel: 403-245-8588
www.frontenachouse.com

As the living ascendants
we acknowledge the roots of our poetic traditions,
and dedicate this anthology to the memory and spirit
of the people, families and communities who are no longer with us
except through their defining works that continue to inspire us.

Editorial Acknowledgements

We are indebted to George Elliott Clarke and Karina Vernon as our consultants and writers on this project. We also extend gratitude to our adviser Alice Major for her detailed and attentive eye and to Rudy Fearon for his help. We are also in appreciation of the many conversations and experiences that we have had with poets and authors in preparation for this anthology.

We appreciate the work of others such as Lorris Elliott, Camilla Haynes, George Elliott Clarke, Afua Cooper, Wayde Compton, Donna Bailey Nurse, ahdri zhina mandiela, Andrea Thompson, Adebe Derango-Adem, Anthony Bansfield, Karen Richardson, Steven Green, the late Ayanna Black and the late Maxine Tynes, all of whom have worked to edit important anthologies. Thank you Ann Horak for your vision of a sisterly press that would serve as a literary spark. Much gratitude for the early conversations, advice and support of Sheri-D Wilson, Peter Midgely and Cheryl Kehoe. We appreciate the support from Black Dot Roots and Culture Collective for helping us see the big picture. Special acknowledgements to Lyn Cadence for marketing and social networking support. And thanks to Harold Head for compiling the first anthology of Black poetry and prose in Canada, *Canada In Us Now* (and to the Rutherford Library based at the University of Alberta, for helping us locate a copy of this ground-breaking book, and for providing us with free photocopying services).

In this anthology we chose to emphasize new and unpublished works by living Canadian poets of African descent, although you will also find a few poems that have been previously published. We hope this collection will connect print poetry with performance poetry across the current generations.

There are of course the special challenges of language and representation that limited our ability as editors to broaden our scope and share all the stories of the African Canadian diaspora. Our original request to receive submissions only in English was made solely on the working language of the editors. However, we realized that we needed to move beyond our first language and invite French speaking poets to submit in French. Most of these poets chose to translate their own work into English before submitting, with one exception, who was happy for us to translate his poem into English. Our particular thanks go to Bruce Strand for his translation. We extend a further thank-you to Deanna Smith and Moe Clark for advising us on Francophone poets, dialects and bilingualism, and to Anthony F. Morgan for his knowledge on the subject, and for helping us to recognize the importance of accepting poems submitted in French. Our hope is that we will find a publisher who will republish this anthology in French, which is the first language of several of the poets in this anthology.

Thank you Michelle Todd, Jennifer Kelly, Nii Tawiah Koney, and Yasmine Coulter for your support of and commitment to this project. Thank you to Edmonton Arts Council for funding a plane flight to Toronto so we could meet with our consultants.

We have much gratitude to Afua Cooper, Dwayne Morgan, Wayde Compton, Klyde Broox, Lillian Allen, John Akpata, Tanya Evanson and Ian Keteku for their interviews and for helping us do the best we can to reflect the multi-faceted culture of Black poets in Canada. We are thankful to Kwame Dawes for sharing his perspective on the fluidity and wholistic nature of poetry across perceived genres. Also a big thank you to Sizwe Adekayode, Wayn Hamilton, El Jones, Pat Kipping, Kathy Fisher, Community Culture and Heritage Nova Scotia, and Western Carnival Development Association, organizers of CARIWEST, Caribbean Arts Festival. We are also proud to be part of Frontenac's eminent list of poetry titles. We also thank the many poets who helped put the word out. And of course thank-you to every poet who had the courage to send us your work—without exception it was a joy to read all your poetry. Much respect to all the poets who have allowed us to publish.

We encouraged poets to choose the genre or style of poetry they felt best represented the poems they selected to submit. Our call for submissions was intended for contributors who identified with African, Afro-Caribbean, African-American, African Canadian or people living in Canada who identify as Black, including indigenous peoples of African descent. We express our full respect for the poets who felt they did not want to be in the anthology because they chose not to self-define as Black or African.

There were many challenges in the selection and preparation of this timely collection of poetry. We did the best we could to create something great with this opportunity. We believe this anthology will add to the canon of Black Poetry throughout the diaspora and to the Canadian poetic tradition. Maxine Tynes, in her poem "The Profile of Africa", reminds us "we wear our skin like a fine fabric"—it is this patchwork quilt of identity, ethnicity and cultural expression that keeps us warm in the winters of the great Canadian north.

Dr. Valerie Mason-John a.k.a. Queenie
Kevan Anthony Cameron a.k.a. Scruffmouth

Contents

STAGE

Dub   105

Spoken Word   141

Slam   195

Preface

It is astonishing to realize, given the flourishing of black cultural production in Canada, especially in the last three decades, that the book you hold in your hands is the first anthology of black Canadian poetry to come out since Harold Head published the earliest such anthology, *Canada in Us Now*, in 1979. Of course, the intervening years have seen a number of anthologies published that transformed Canada's literary landscape in powerful ways, including Lorris Elliott's *Other Voices: Writings by Blacks in Canada* (1985); George Elliott Clarke's two-volume *Fire on the Water* (1991-1992); Ayanna Black's *Fiery Spirits: Canadian Writers of African Descent* (1994); Djanet Sears's *Testifying: Contemporary African Canadian Drama* (2000); Wayde Compton's *Blueprint: Black British Columbian Literature and Orature* (2001) and Donna Bailey Nurse's *Revival: An Anthology of Black Canadian Writing* (2006). All these anthologies have helped to recover and delineate the field of black Canadian letters, each in its own particular and important way, but significantly, none is national in its perspective, and none focuses specifically on the genre of poetry. The publication of *Great Black North*, then, offers an opportunity to reflect on what has changed in the intervening three and a half decades since the publication of *Canada in Us Now*. Where is black Canada today? Who are its poets and what are its current poetics?

Much has changed since 1979 and, for better and for worse, much has also stayed the same. Two generations of black Canadian poets have come to prominence since 1979; these younger generations have placed an emphasis on local and regional forms of Canadian blackness that we don't yet see expressed in Head's anthology, which remains largely Toronto-centric. Poets such as Wayde Compton, Bertrand Bickersteth, and David Woods are articulating how particular local geographies, histories and literary traditions, in British Columbia, Alberta, and Nova Scotia, inflect black subjectivity and black expression in unique ways. This, then, is perhaps the first anthology with a truly national scope, since the poets included here represent—with full self awareness—the diverse range of regional blacknesses that have been produced in Canada.

There are other signal differences between the poets selected here and those represented in Head's anthology. Unlike the poets of 1979, contemporary black Canadian poets have the benefit of a well-mapped and lengthy Canadian literary tradition, thanks to the efforts of a number of writers and scholars to excavate black Canadian history and literature. Whereas Head notes in his Introduction that "the writers in this anthology were schooled in Shakespeare, Wordsworth, Blake, Byron,

Shelley, Keats and Browning," young poets today are able to draw on the vital tradition of work by black Canadian writers, from Mifflin Wistar Gibbs and Frederick Ward, to Austin Clark, Claire Harris and M. NourbeSe Philip. Contemporary poets are also more aware of their deep national, regional, and diasporic black histories.

Frequently in this collection, poets return to history—to Marie Joseph Angélique; to the history of Africville; to John Ware and the black history of the prairies—in order to locate a self and a poetic voice in relation to the history that conditions and underwrites them.

It is difficult to overstate the difference that the various historical and literary recovery projects of the last thirty years have made to the tradition of black poetry in Canada. Black Canadian poetry in 1979, according to Harold Head, was "a return, in spirit, to origins, to Africa where the work of the artist is even today at one with his community and where his work is validated and legitimized by this community itself." Today, black Canadian poets are still interested in the continent and its political, textual and oral traditions, along with those of the diaspora. But a number of the poets in this collection are turning away from the "from-ness" of claiming the self as other, as foreign to Canada, in order to assert a new kind of "here-ness," however tentatively. As Anthony Joyette writes:

> I am no longer an
> exotic dish of this or that,
> but everything they are.
> Cold humour and warm wishes,
> Fashioned by the arms of diversity.
> More they, than what I used to be.

Along similar lines, Wayde Compton writes:

> I stand in the penumbra of myself, my eyes
> Neruda was tired of his shadow, I'm
> of the response and call numb
> the lung undone come mumbling up off
> the floor of the ocean for no
> holy corona of from.

Black Canadian poets and scholars have done much to bring our histories and literatures out into the light, but that does not necessarily mean that the Canadian terrains of race, power, culture, politics and privilege have become easier for us to negotiate. There is a sense in this anthology that Canada remains, for the black subject and poet, difficult ground. As David Woods eloquently writes, "In my voyage of discovery/ I push through the blurred/ landscape not yet mastered."

Despite the changes in black Canadian poetry and poetics in the last three decades, much remains the same. What Harold Head wrote in 1979 about black Canadian poetry being rooted in an essentially oral tradition remains just as true in our own cultural moment. "Black literature springs from a still vital oral culture," writes Head. "The close interaction between creator and audience, artist and community is perhaps the single most important element in black literature, especially poetry." But to Head's list of black musical forms—"jazz, spirituals, funeral dirges, work-songs, calypsos, limbo, church hollers, reggae, rhythm and blues, freedom marches, soul"—we now must add hip-hop. A new generation of performance poets is today strengthening the oral dimension of black Canadian poetry with dub and slam performances. One of the most bracing things about reading this anthology is the way that—by including the current generation of slam and performance poets—its editors Valerie Mason-John and Kevan Cameron complicate our assumptions about what poetry is and what poetry does, who makes it, who reads and who hears it.

Great Black North is an essential contribution to our living literary tradition, one that is over two hundred years in the making.

Karina Vernon
Toronto, July 2012

Exceptional Poetics

For Maxine Tynes (1949-2011)

To read African-Canadian poetry is to encounter exceptional poetics—in terms of the African Diaspora and in terms of the Anglo-Canadian literary canon. Africans elsewhere may perceive Canada—as do many Canadians—as being a Caucasian, Nordic realm, with a European monarch, and an insignificant black population, who don't really "belong," but whose presence adds a decorative accent to multicultural, "tourism" marketing. Of course, African-Canadian voices, within the African Diaspora, must also constitute a minority persuasion. No one could be blamed for thinking of "African-Canadian poetry" as a preposterous entry in an encyclopedia of world literature.

Too, African–heritage poets and Anglo-Canadian verse make odd bedfellows. Indeed, white, Anglo-Canadian poetry has been marked by a predilection for intellectual statement and disdain for "popular" movements. Moreover, these poets have preferred nature observation to socio-political engagement. In short, Anglo-Canadian poetry's elitist orientation is cold to the "performance" aesthetic that animates many African-Canadian poets and the peoples they claim as their own. While Caucasian Canadian poets are often pleased to stress classicism and hieratic, hermetic (post) modernism, many black poets choose to preach and teach, uplift or upset, sing and "swing," all with reacting listeners in mind, not just silent readers. Thus, though Canada is a hierarchical society, with its orders of this and that, black poets tend to be more populist. The reason is that black song and sermon, slang and folklore, remain just as important to us as do the Caucasian canons served up in classrooms. Also vital is "voice." Self-conscious—or *conscious*—or conscientious black poets extend a tradition where the voice and the body (feet and hands) comprise instruments of expression that are equal to—or, at times, supersede—the printed word. For black poets, the "paper" poem may be so much flimsy whimsy compared to the word that is shouted or whispered, spoken or sung. For us, the "staged" recital, depending on "flow" or "rap"—the patter or rat-a-tat-tat of ideas and images, is just as essential as phrases set down, secured in ink, but living as *cadence*. Ultimately, the difference between most "black" poets and most "white" poets in Canada is that "performance"—I mean, the relationship to a live audience—registers as more important for us than publication and reception by unknown readers who may or may not "get" the references ....

In a culture which values elitism, ecological critique, and *über* education, what is the black poet to say or write that is simultaneously Canadian and distinctly rooted in the African Diaspora? I think the answer is here in the pages of this anthology, but it is also an answer that has been given, consistently, albeit in fits and starts, over the four hundred years of African people's presence in Nouvelle France and British America, and then in British North America and Canada, on what was—and still is, *really,* First Nations' soil. (Columbus be damned!) It has to do with who we are, where we are, when and how we arrived, and from whence we came. Thus, the tracts and spirituals of African-Nova Scotian Baptists insist that "God ... brought us a mighty long way" or recall meetings in fields and forests, spirituals sung among stony land and snowy wastes. The black settler narratives of the last century recall efforts to build farm communities on the Prairies, safe from lynch mobs, if not mosquitoes. Check out executed slave Marie-Josèphe Angélique's coerced confession in which she testifies to her attempt to run away from Montréal, struggling through snow, to try to reach freedom in Vermont. Like all Canadians, black writers here also grapple with the facts of climate and geography, though *perhap*s with a greater spiritual connection to a history of struggle for liberty and equality. Yet, in comparison with African-American poets, African-Canadian poets have also tended to be, like Anglo-Canadian poets as a whole, more abstract. See now the first African-Canadian poetry collections—by a man and a woman—in English. I refer to Robert Nathaniel Dett's *Album of a Heart* (1911) and Anna Minerva Henderson's *Citadel* (1967).

Album of a Heart, published in Jackson, Tennessee, is instructive for an inquiry into the poetics of African-Canadian verse. Raised in Drummondville—now Niagara Falls, Ontario, Dett (1882-1943) is significant to African-American musicology, for, as a scholar of the Negro spiritual, he published two historic compilations: *Religious Folk-Songs of the Negro as Sung at Hampton Institute* (1927) and *The Dett Collection of Negro Spirituals* (1936). Importantly, Dett launches (or follows) several African-Canadian tendencies. *Album of a Heart* utilizes "dialect" and standard English—just as our Black Canadian poets do in this volume. The poem "Conjured" is practically ragtime in rhythm:

Couldn't sleep last night!
Just toss and pitch!
I'm conjured! I'm conjured!
By that little witch!
… Whenever I try to think;
Side track and switch
My thoughts do; and finally
Dump me in the ditch.

The diction is ragged too, more related to blues and the brothel than to the college where Dett was ensconced when his book was published. Yet, in the same volume as "Conjured," there is the stately, Tennysonian "At Niagara":

No! No! Not tonight, my Friend,
I may not, cannot go with you tonight.
And think not that I love you any less
Because this now I'd rather be alone.

The poem is rather mysterious; it could be about spiritual disaffection, homoerotic confusion, or suicidal brooding:

Urge me no further, now that you understand.
A nobler friend than you none ever knew
But not this time. Tonight I'll be alone ….

In "Pappy," Dett covers the then-popular Plantation tradition in American poetry: "When I was a pickaninny / many years ago, / I members how my mammy used ter call me …" One can almost imagine Al Jolson, in blackface, performing this "number." But, being Canadian, Dett produces "Au Matin"—a bit of drivel about ghostly dawns and gone love—and also "Au Soir,"which, being a better poem, salutes copulation:

Now does joy
Its bounds transcend—
Would the night
Might never end!
O soft shine on us
From above,
Beauteous Night
Of perfect love.

So, there you have it: The first African-Canadian "book" poet authors pop-song-styled lyrics, formal verse, alludes to French, and indulges in dialect verse. In addition, Dett was an expatriate intellectual, pursuing a career in the United States, presumably because there was no room for him in Canada—the Great White North. A composer as well as a scholar, he remains a crucial Harlem Renaissance figure in the United States, but is remembered here mainly in the prestigious, Toronto-based, eponymous Nathaniel Dett Chorale.

The first African-Canadian woman to publish a book of poems was Anna Minerva Henderson (1887-1987), who was a retired civil servant, aged 80, when her chapbook, *Citadel*, appeared in the Canadian Centennial year, in Saint John, New Brunswick. A New Brunswicker by birth, she was a stellar pupil—really, an intellectual—in a time of few serious educational opportunities for blacks in general and black women in particular. Indeed, Henderson obtained a teacher's certificate, taught school in Nova Scotia, and then, in 1912, at age 25, was hired into the federal civil service after writing an entrance test and earning the third highest grade in Canada. While in Ottawa, she wrote a column for the *Ottawa Citizen* titled "The Colyum" or "Just Among Ourselves." By the time she was 50, Henderson was publishing her verse in journals. When Henderson self-published *Citadel*, a slim booklet of 31 pages, she did not compose either a "collected" or a "selected" poems. Rather, *Citadel* is a crafted chapbook focused on Saint John's cityscape and history, the British connection, faith, and the strife between artist and critic: It is neither a hodgepodge of musings nor a select batch of the author's "best." Instead, it must be considered her forceful entry into her city's literary culture, though it is doubtful that most readers would have known the author was black. Henderson's poems are mainly sonnets or quatrains; seldom does she allow free verse to darken her pages. She comments on Loyalist history, the foggy look and soggy feel of Saint John, and, almost never, on race and racism. The key to Henderson's low-key style is "Mount Mansfield, Vermont": In this sonnet, the speaker exults in climbing the mountain—in a ski resort—and feels "singing happiness." Her exultation prefaces the claim, "This now we know— / That nevermore can level valley-ways / Shrouded in mist and sheltered far below, / Suffice to hold us captive through our days." Superficially, the speaker is pleased to be at the summit of a redoubtable mountain, and feels that she may repeat the experience. But, in solid metaphysical tradition, Henderson moves the poem toward allegory: "And in the valley, dark in dreams below / Gleam here and there the twinkling lights of Stowe." As it turns out, the Vermont resort is named after Harriet Beecher Stowe, whose *Uncle Tom's Cabin* (1852) served to ignite the American Civil War. Most subtly, Henderson is likening the mountain climb (prescient of Rev. Dr. Martin Luther King's imagery in his final sermon of April 3, 1968) to the dream of freedom once held by slaves, who looked to abolitionists like Stowe for inspiration. But the successful "escapee," now at the summit, basks in the moon's "floods of silver light."

I think the examples of Dett and Henderson pave the way for the poets and poems that follow here. Arguably, African-Canadian poetics is multicultural, polyphonic, vernacular, intellectual, interested in geopolitical history and spirituality, and allusive—to black speech and song as much as it is to the printed canon. Enter, all ye now, into the *Great Black North* ....

George Elliott Clarke, O.C., O.N.S., Ph.D.
E.J. Pratt Professor of Canadian Literature
University of Toronto

PAGE

Print Poetry

Based on interviews by Valerie Mason-John
with Afua Cooper and Wayde Compton

Few poets are commercially published and even fewer Black poets. However, the legendary ones include some of Canada's best poets in print—writers like Olive Senior, Claire Harris, Dionne Brand (winner of the 2011 Griffin Prize), George Elliott Clarke, Wayde Compton, Afua Cooper, M. NourbeSe Philip, Frederick Ward, Lorna Goodison, Pamela Mordecai and Shane Book. There is also a long list of African Canadian / Black Canadian poets who see themselves as "print poets" but who are not yet published in book form. All are paying attention to detail, to what the poem looks like on the page, to using traditional poetic forms as part of their craft.

The category of print poetry is problematic, and defining it will depend on who you are talking to. In a print-dominated culture, the published book is often considered to be the "real poetry", with performance a subsidiary. In fact, print poetry is an extension of the oral tradition and much of what is recorded on the page is about preserving, documenting, and recording the oral tradition so it does not get lost. Black Canadian poets often engage with the whole page-performance range in their work.

Dr. Afua Cooper is a scholar, poet and author of *The Hanging of Angélique: The Untold Story of Slavery in Canada and the Burning of Old Montréal* (a national best-seller nominated for the Governor General's Award in 2006). She describes page poetry as "putting lines and words on the page as they would be spoken."

Cooper adds, "The challenge is how you put the voice on the page. This can be a beautiful tension because you are always thinking of new ways to be engaging. Those who have the creative tension between the voice and the page are at the vanguard of Canadian poetry."

Wayde Compton, an essayist, author and poet, says, "I was reading my poetry anywhere who would have me. When my poetry collection *49th Parallel Psalm* came out in 1999, people stopped calling me a spoken word poet, and I became a page poet."

Compton was influenced by Dionne Brand and George Elliott Clarke. "I found these writers when I was trying to orient myself. I loved George Elliott Clarke's *Salt Water Spirituals and Deeper Blues*. I loved that he was writing about the long-standing Black communities in Canada."

Much of Black poetry in Canada is rooted in particular historical experiences such as that of the Black Loyalists, the African slaves sold in Nova Scotia during the 1700s, the arrival of the Maroons in 1796, the settlement of Africville in Halifax in the early 1800s, the coming of the Fugitives (the thousands of slaves who arrived in southern Ontario via the Underground Railroad in the 1850s), the many African-Americans who settled in Victoria, British Colombia in 1858. Each province, and city has a different story to tell, harkening back to 1603 when Mathieu Da Costa, a free Black man, set foot on Canadian soil and worked as a translator of English, French, Dutch, Portuguese, Pidgin Basque (the dialect of many Aboriginals used for trading purposes.) Twenty-five years later the first named African slave, a six-year-old boy, is recorded as residing in Canada. Today provinces like Ontario, Quebec, Nova Scotia, Alberta and British Columbia host large African Canadian, Black Canadian communities in Canada.

"It's hard being Black in Canada," says Cooper. "There is such a denial of racism—a denial around native and Black people. As poets we have a role to be political for as long as we are oppressed and subjugated. Poetry will continue and as poets, whether page or spoken word, we have to rediscover our mission. We are the chronicles of experience, the voice of the poor and the dispossessed."

Many younger poets, who like Cooper and Compton began in dub or spoken-word, have been greatly influenced by internationally acclaimed print poets like Dionne Brand and George Elliott Clarke. Their books are the ones that they find in the libraries. Their words on the page are part of the rich tapestry of African-Canadian, Black Canadian history and culture.

AFUA COOPER

Confessions of a Woman Who Burnt Down a Town
Based on the last days of Marie-Joseph Angélique[1]

I buried the twins that evening
they died of smallpox
were only 8 months old
Madame came too to the funeral
and said to me by way of consolation
"c'est la vie,
I too have lost my own."
I went back to work
went back to work in Madame's house
that same evening and at supper she yelled at me
and box me full in the face because
I overturned the gravy bowl in her lap

I remember my journey too from my island to this island
from Madeira to Manhattan to Montreal
Monsieur bought me on one of his business trips
He said I looked like a healthy wench
He died soon after, and Madame never forgave me
but I had nothing to do with it, he died of consumption

The twins died too.
After we buried them that evening
my heart changed position in my chest
and I was seized with one desire and one desire only
and that was to leave the prison of this island
But where could I go
Because, throughout the whole world
in all the continents people who look like me
were bound
But still, all I could see was
my feet running, no chains, no rope, no shackles
free

Madame talking to her best friend
and confessor Father Labadie
"I'm going to sell that negress, she's getting too much
for me, she's getting too uppity
And furthermore since Francois died I just can't seem to manage
Look for a buyer for me father, perhaps the church is interested."
I bring in the food and pretend like ah neva hear
and I serve the food good and proper
was on my best behaviour
roll back mi lip and skin mi teeth
roll back my yai and show the white
den I went back to mi room in the cellar
and mek mi plan

Smoke, smoke, too much smoke
only intend fi one house fi burn
fire, fire, too much fire
but it done go so already
and I running
my feet unshackled, unbound,
free
running pass di city limits
while behind me the fire rage
and my raging heart change back into its rightful position

He was running too
Claude Thibault
this salt smuggler, prisoner, soldier, from France
I gave him all my food to take me to or show me
the way to New England but he tek the food
and leave me while I was sleeping
an the constables caught me

I don't utter a word as I sit here in the jailhouse
Father Labadie come to confess me
but I refuse
their god is not my god
"Arson is one of the worst crime in New France Marie,"
he say to me, "confess now and save your soul."

I spit on the ground
outside, the mob want to rip me from limb to limb
but I not afraid, a strange calm fill my body
and I at peace, peace, perfect peace

Guilty, the judge pronounce
and the sentence: to be tortured, my hands cut off
my body burned and the ashes scattered
to the four corners of the earth
I break down, my body crumple in a heap
and before my eyes I see the twins
and they look so alive as if they waiting
for me to come nurse them
The sentence is reduced
Now dem jus goin to hang me and den burn mi body
Father Labadie come back for di confession
And I confess
is I Marie who set the fire
I say yes
I start it in Madame's house by the river
50 building destroy
the hospital, the cathedral
I confess
is I Marie who burn this city
so write that down Father Labadie
write down my story so it can be known in history
with my heart burning I take the sacrament
and accept the final rites
outside the guard is waiting
to take me to my hanging
outside the guard is waiting to take me to my dying
outside the guard in waiting to take me to my burning
Soon I will be free from the prison of this island
and I will fly and fly and fly

petit oiseau, s'envoler.

WAYDE COMPTON

Loxodromic

a voice is a box of reaping, a dream
a dicotyledon of speaking.
unlocking makes purchase by re-revealing
submarine cables. coloured, keening,
sung
krakens, reeling,
role and role out a whole cracking Occident.

from the moon's floor to the bight of thinking,
from the seeding descent to the shell of telegraphy,

of Valentia Island to Trinity Bay,
of a breathless expression,
a last westless east, a leached hereless list
for this low slow
perch of hiss

as though through the throats
of a dole of punctuating rock doves—

> [Paul Reuter flew pigeons released stock threw air
> from Brussels to Aachen for a falling
> of figures on wings of flushing vestige
> through solid moulting into air threw
> temporal ink the invisible digits
> went where a whistle opts not to centre]

I stand in the penumbra of myself, my eyes
Neruda was tired of his shadow, I'm
of the response and call numb
the lung undone come mumbling up off
the floor of the ocean for no
holy corona of from.

Valentia Island to Trinity Bay
Brussels to Aachen

[Alex Haley tracked the word across the written in
saline keel quill stole to Juffere away
from Spotsylvania and back to where the occult griot
opened up in him an ink sea of pages in confidence
evidence on the plage the word The
African cowry game traces the helix flown long
the god that owns the word is always a huckster
a river a banjo a name a season a word is a skinless drum]

west I go as the crazed crows commute
east, singing at one hundred and ten km per hour "I'm
Looking Through You" twice through, confused
as to whether I'm lead or backing,
Saul as the storytelling actually seems to fall
out of the sun, as I break apart from
Coquitlam, the paved name of native slaves of natives
set free too far from home to go

again, a twister of tricksters I see against
this con of a sun. they descend against
sequence and "You Keep Me Hangin' On"
on Boundary Road northbound until the streets
drive the history back to an accident of contact.

[shotgun to Manhattan from Montreal I read the road map as she
drove
and all I could see was lyrical time in the boxed lines flying]

GEORGE ELLIOTT CLARKE

From "Canticles": *First Christmas*

Watching *Star*-ignited snow sparkle,
Herod unleashes a cranky butchering:
Romans must rip open Hebrew skin—
distinguish circumcised babes
and extinguish them,
so they perish
amid spasms of shitting.

Legions will root out all infants
showing "cat-sly or bright, marble eyes."

To scoop up gold, troops must set blood a-flood.

Before they put beer in their bellies,
they must toss kiddos into infernos.

Herod's frothing and spittle expound
his gross appetite for Hebrew grief.
He nods; he points; he shrugs.

Squads scurry to assassinate "brats,"
to nitpick shadow-chequered alleys,
to enjoy pirates' raptures,
this ice-delighting December,
and slay and slay
until *Weariness* overtakes each day.

After games of cat-and-mouse,
it's dog-eat-dog,
eye-for-eye and tooth-for-tooth,
death-for-all and all-for-death:
Babes are axed, knifed, bludgeoned, stomped on,
and flung into fires.

It is genocide
from the ground up;
it's a down-to-earth roll-call
of scorched-earth massacre.

Children are splayed and speared
amid hay, pine needles, and dirt,
or stabbed on shit-browned snow.
It's a ruddy reaping, eh?

Soldiers plump on gold cut from baby fat.
They tooth and tear—
as in *Tragedy*.
Rending guts, they render kids' bellies sausages—
stinking, but tasty to dogs.
Damn! They bed down in gore.

Then, the sword-and-sandal bastards pass around
sugary plonk in trophy cups,
splash purple drink into big-ass, silver bowls.
Sanguine is that wine.

(*War* yields *Fame* and yawning *Infamy*.)

But the Roman swords prove worthless.
The divine chile's flit o'er to Egypt.

Halifax (Nova Scotia) 3 mai mmxii

DAVID WOODS

The New Chapter
for Africville

Sometimes, in the flood of words
I return to the black houses …
tarpaper shacks,
And solemn lives walking the
old, stone road.

Big Town … Southwestern …
Round The Turn …
Sacred spots on the map,
And new routes in my voyage
of discovery.

I fork through grey shale … blood pines,
Into the sooty landscape not yet
mastered by my hands.
Climbing the steep hilltop
to peer into village life below.

To see a yellow house
opened like a womb,
And Aunt Ruth still there
awaiting my return—
To continue her tale of lives
that swerve through the mist outside,
Or walk magically along the train tracks

That since her death
flood my pen like blood.

OLIVE SENIOR

They're Stoning The Mango Tree Again

They're stoning the mango tree again.
Puny fruits and leaves shower down like rain.
The best of the crop has retreated to the top
of the tree and out of reach and no one
dares to breach the rampart of ancient trunk
and limbs armed with spiky wild pines
and stinging ants. Still they come, the army
of mango scavengers, with sticks and stones
and the heavy artillery of the fallen branch.
The bottom half is nearly bare of fruit now
and the reapers grow increasingly frantic.

Get a life I want to yell at them. Or, find
another mango tree. If this one were to
charge for her services, with so many
solicitations all day long, she'd be a rich bitch.

Instead, from my window, I have the last
laugh. As soon as the reapers have vanished
for the day, the feathered residents
come to stay. Soon I'll hear over and over
the BIF-BOOF sounds of mangoes dropping
from the topmost limbs and hitting the ground.
Ripe mangoes laughing and rolling around.

By tomorrow when the reapers return to
retrieve this fallen treasure, the birds,
the wasps, the flies and the worms
would have dined at leisure.

Killer Bees

This is not a pretty picture. This is a picture of a girl
pushed to the edge by a wedge of her schoolmates.
This is a crowd shot, a loud shot of laughter and hate.

What is the scent, the flower that blooms inside of her
that attracts the killer bees?

M. NOURBESE PHILIP

big questions

                           why does a chicken always cross a road
       and b follow a when the worm turns why
                  don't we tell it like it was and what
         did you say the time
                     was when the zebra changed
          its stripes and is it true
                        what they say who is
       they did humpty
              dumpty jump or was he
                   pushed when led to the water
     why didn't the horse drink why
                 isn't the earth flat and how do you
close
        a basket case when you say I am and
               how do you say you are can
        you kill three birds
   with one stone when the
                   birds in the bush seduce
       the one in your
           hand

Flagelliform # 13: Night Births

Fear of the wicks. Fear of the sacred creamy air.
Fear of the debriefings on precisely which sweet
know-nothings were blown into him. Which
is a question he swells within. Which, he holds
the dark lantern to, and thus. Thus reveals
the sung-dread of the receding trail. Dread
of breaching the sign warning of snowberries.
Dread of the sliding place. Awe of the night
disease. Awe of the waste-part remaining.
Awe of the dog child's heavings. A dog child's
stitching gait. His dark red hog, his brindled
hog tongue. An earless dog of the earless ones.
A dog an offering for the hammer mechanism.
Palatable is the sacrifice for the pitted tusk. ·
Pitiful in the redness without cover. Pitiful
in his muskgarment. "I go naked on the way
to Bolga." Where the adobe weapons end
in septums. From the hooks and the searing.
From the splaying and the quiet. The tunneling
wind through his wet cage. Younger brother
of the earless ones, those Afrogothic. Out
from a giant growth come a noise. Out from
a pustular growth come a hanging. Out from
a jaundiced growth come the tail swinging its
length. Out from a pulsing growth come
the ash-smudged necks. Born in the time
when clay pots dotted his carrion farms.
"I bind the glowing worm in the forehead."

SUZETTE MAYR

Aunt Rosel

This inevitable thing. This fright.
This mordant verdant redundant inclement nighttime daytime
endless train track thing.
This twilight this dusk this filth this cancerous fact this boredom this
morphine sleep this morphine addict this lump that won't digest.

My aunt can still chew a lump or two of gorgonzola pizza. A fork
stab to her mouth. But she prefers cigarettes. Shot glasses of cherry
liqueur.

Her cigarette smoke tamps down on us in this bell jar. Lucky Strike.
Cigarettes Kill You. Cigarettes Cause Ageing of the Skin. Cigarettes
Cause Lung Cancer. Cigarettes Cause Mouth Diseases. Tobacco
Makes You Impotent. Cigarettes Are Consolation. Cigarettes Make
Grieving Boring.

A cigarette propped in her hand, thickening column of ash
head nodding forward her fading perm & auburn dye job. She is 60.

This creaking of the floor the door this shutting of the room thing
she creeps from bedroom bathroom bedroom
creak of the bed the door the floor while we wait in this terminal.

Chum

I love my friend the way I love a carbuncle, a hardened pimple, a
ripe ingrown hair. I love her the way I love the black spot in the
palm of my hand, a pencil tip I stabbed myself with, that accidental
imprint. I love her the way I love the recurring eczema patches on
my eyelids, the hard chunks of wax in my itchy ears, the dry skin
flakes I scrape off my scalp with the cap from my pen, bonk bonk bonk
my heel hitting the floor in dog-scratch ecstasy. I love her the
way I love the grease shine on my forehead, my sinus flare-ups in
the company of cats, dust, grass. I love her like my fibroid tumour,
that knuckle jammed into the wall of my uterus. I love her the way I
love my leaking period, that reassuring trickle and blood pour a
brown panty scrub in the bathroom sink. I love her the way I love
that muscle gnarl between my shoulder blades, that bunion beneath
my left big toe, that split nail on my right index finger, pointing to
how much I love her.

AHDRI ZHINA MANDIELA

brownsun (i dance a wheel)

ever/y/time/i see/me dance
i dance/where i dance/i dance
a speak/my feet/sound/ing/top my
dancing feet: sing in/to my heart

and then some-
times/i must find/my own way
open my own day/ignite my/brown
sun/dance my own sun/round my
dancing/spinning parts

and when i/dance
my rhythm toes/feel like
dance/spinning toes
beneath my tongue & teeth/singing
flows/beneath my dancing wheel
feels like brown/sun/singing
streams/on my brown sun/spinning
wheels

and then some-
times/i must find my own/way/
then/i may/splay/my rhythm/toes
ignite my frozen woes/let
my heart go/where? it goes

and yes some-
times/i must find/my own/way
my/own/brown sun/play/my own
(slap/slap/hands/slap)
hands & feet play/hide
& find my own/brown
sun/my own/brown fun
(slap hands/slap hands)
make my own/brown sun
wake my own brown/find my own/brown
/feel my own/brown/i can/feel brown/

i can feel/my own brown/sun/feel my own
i can/brown/sun/makes me feel
/i can/brown sun
makes me feel/i can dance

from/here/to the end/of my brown sun
(i dance a wheel)

JULIANE OKOT BITEK

Diaspora

I can't make it,
The note said
So she sent flowers in her stead

I can't make it
There's a fire in the sink
The dog is barking
The children have run away
There's a run in my stocking
Laundry to be done
The stench of burned eggs
A cigarette butt in the geraniums
And breaking news on TV

I can't make it
The note said
So she sent flowers instead
Flowers would have to do
They were a mixed bunch
Colourful, playful
Each complimenting the other
Each louder, then softer
They sang a beautiful song

She couldn't make it, she said in her note
So she sent flowers instead
Red, white, yellow and pink
And the odd one dyed blue, green, orange
Soft, sweet and twenty-four
Still yearning, still believing in the right to be
They were hacked at their slender necks
Stuffed in clear plastic
Bound with blue satin
And handed over with panache and a smile

She couldn't make it
She said in her note
So she sent a bunch of flowers
Sat on the couch
And imagined the hacked dead of the Congo
Flash against the screen

GEORGE AUGUSTO BORDEN

Black Athletes

Seeds of Spartan fathers—
planted in the vineyards of love …
nurtured from the rains of Mother Africa:
roots of rebirth,
blossoms of beauty,
flowers of fortune.

Gems of Amazon mothers—
adorned in a veneer of ebony …
polished in the ways of Kunta-land:
pearls of pride,
jewels of justice,
diamonds of destiny.

Born of Hamite stock—
suckled at the fountain of hope …
modeled after strengths of yester-year:
daring of Harriet Tubman,
spirit of Sojourner Truth,
conviction of Frederick Douglass.

Fruits from nature's orchard—
plucked from the branches of life …
preserved along the "passage" of death:
food for fashion,
treats of pleasure,
banquets for gluttons.

Heirs to a mighty legacy—
descendants of warrior kings …
children of a greater god:
trustees of time,
executors of excellence,
beneficiaries of Blackness.

LORNA GOODISON

Aunt Rose

Our favorite photograph shows her in a blush-pink
Parisian spring suit. Observe the soft felt cloche,
the high-heeled shoes, tendrils of suede straps
x-ing across insteps, kissing her long narrow feet.

Damask Rose, too gorgeous, reduced sincere men
to silence. They'd end up drumming nervous digits
on taut throat-skins, attempting to tap out wooing
messages, appropriate toasts to the Rose of Sharon.

Even in Montreal, where gilded French women
would go, exalted by haute couture, she'd cause
Quebecois men to groan "moo dieu" and plunge off
street cars calling "comment s'appelle Main'selle?"

Beauty concentrated, top to base note she trailed.
A human pomander, the very particles and waves
of her roseate self would scent odourless atoms.
Her essence permeating skin, blood, bones, flesh,

she drew in breath and blew out rosewater scent.
Fragrance-deficient ones begged caresses from her
scented hands which in the end became coated
with attar of Roses. Attar yes, Rose knew burnings,

but the fair Rose of Jericho, never wanting to speak
of such scorchings, would press down her torched
voicebox, scarred and keloid with beauty burns,
to the last releasing rose scents, but no sounds.

Aunt Alberta

Amazing how Aunt Alberta was named by an act
of sheer prescience after a Province of Canada. Alberta,
born 1903 on the island of Jamaica,

one Easter morning cracked an egg and sighted a ship
becalmed between yolk and albumen. Taking a hint,
she boarded a steamer and sailed

faraway from life in a sun-lit green Jamaican village
founded by her grandfather into a city of ice storms.
No lingua franca but the tongue

of Quebecois, and unaccustomed hard labor in Mont Royal.
She lived in service, taking orders; a saint remitting
money and care-parcels for an entire village.

Photographs show her dolorous in snow banks, solitary
in deep sylvan glades of photo studios, till at aged forty-
four she married one Geoffrey Seal,

a Barbadian, himself stone-faced in service, first and only
man to uncover her loveliness. It came unexpected,
Aunt Alberta's late luck, in the form

of a tender companion who wore her wool scarves
like prayer shawls, holy her barely-scented handkerchiefs.
He slept, telling her pearls like a rosary.

FREDERICK WARD

No School Today
A Teacher's Lament

800+ Children swallowed
And rest beneath earthquake rubble in Pakistan
O, say, "They had wings", for:

Unsure steps,
When planted in certain mud,
Leave not a trace of self presence,
Present

No school today

Unknown Numbers of
Unfortunate children sucked of breath
Beneath a massive mudslide in Guatemala
O, say, 'They had wings'

No school today

In New Orleans, children
Struggled through floodwaters: top'd by
Oil slick that hiss' of waste, and
Their own tears for a baby's body—*floating*—his relentless hand
Grasped permanently to the tail of a snake
That Hiss'sss,
                    "What tows it?"
Whilst following in the wake of
The children's tiny efforts to escape … towards …
O, say, "They have wings," for:

"Their feet be swept,"
Through dawn's dew on green grass,
Washed:
That freshness attend
Their prayers

ANDREA THOMPSON

A Brief History of Soul Speak

Seemingly innocent spirituals[1]
to both master and overseer
they were merely words
simple lyrics, ingenuous
halleluiah ballads.

Swing low sweet chariot
Coming for to carry me home[2]

But these words were charms
incantations chanted
in secret freedom code
surreptitious melodies
sung by restless slaves
chariot became train
became a rumbling
underground
echoing over plantation field
of cotton, tobacco and cane.

Gospels, for safety
for shouts—never mind battle cries
would leave a nigger dead cold in a heartbeat.

Mothers with babies, strapped to their bent to near
snapped backs, sung under
the unrelenting sun of the Old South
and men with bodies worked hard, then raw
till they were little more than meat and bone
recounted these so-called silly spirituals, to both
each other and God.

God, they asked for strength
each other, they asked for directions
where to cross over that river
where to board that subterranean
north-bound train to freedom.

Then came the blues
belting out anguish over injustice
after emancipation failed
to deliver the promised land
instead, sending Klansmen
who strung-up till lifeless
one brother after another
as law enforcers turned away
and crosses burned till dawn.

Dallas Blues, Memphis Blues[3]
I ain't had nothin but bad news.
Crazy Blues.[4]

Unabashed, these words
laid claim to the pain of generations
love was sought, found, then
—gone, gone, gone
Ye shall overcome if ye faint not[5]
our victory will not be undone.

And so the young entered, at their peril
the guarded gates of academia
living the vision of Booker T. Washington
where scholarly success meant abandoning
one's own language, meant
adopting the mother tongue
of Uncle Tom.

When a hunger for our own vernacular
mingled with the passion of romanticism
a new language was born, on the page
on the stages of smoky coffee houses
deep in the heart of Harlem.

In this Renaissance, we began to reclaim ourselves.

Began to own our newly found freedom
to simply read and write, en masse
in public, to make love and meaning
from our suffering, to live out loud
word by word, on our own terms.

Langston left a language
deep as the Euphrates[6]
that flowed into the ocean
of Gwendolyn, bestowing
permission for preachment
as Baraka and Sanchez
re-loaded the cannon[7]
with unapologetic verse
fueled by didacticism.

And up here, in the true
north beyond that 49th parallel
Clifton Joseph, Devon Haughton
and the indomitable Lillian Allen
waged a Rub-a-Dub revolution
George Elliott Clarke taught us
the maritime equation of
Black + Acadia = Africadian
and Wayde Compton mapped
the path of B.C. Bluesprint.[8]

While across the country
Slam and Hip Hop brought
Rhythm-And-Poetry
back to the streets, and
ghetto speak became fodder
for heightened verbal artistry.

These are our ancestors of verse.
This is our legacy.

And still this history is incomplete
so diverse is the lineage
unsung are so many
who first spoke the words
that birthed the language
of my Soul Speak.

Notes:

i   As slave songs came to be known.

ii   According to The Library of Congress copyright office, the author
     of "Swing Low, Sweet Chariot's" is officially unknown, yet many
     historians site the author as Wallis Willis, a Choctaw freedman in
     the old Indian Territory, sometime before 1862.

iii Hart Wand, "Dallas Blues" (1912), W. C. Handy, "The Memphis
     Blues" (1912).

iv   Italicized lyrics from "Crazy Blues" by Perry Bradford. The first
     African American to create a recording was Mamie Smith, with her
     cover of the song in 1920.

v   Inspiration for the 60s protest song "We shall Overcome", "I'll
     Overcome Some Day" was a hymn written by the Reverend Charles
     Albert Tindley. Epigraph from the published text reads: "Ye shall
     overcome if ye faint not", a quote derived from Galatians 6:9.

vi   Reference to: Langston Hughes' "The Negro Speaks of Rivers". *The
     Weary Blues* (1926)

vii "re-loading the can(n)on" from Klyde Broox' *My Best Friend is
     White* (McGilligan Books, 2005)

viii *Blueprint: Black British Columbian Literature and Orature*,
     anthology edited by Wayde Compton (Arsenal Pulp Press, 2003)

SYLVIA HAMILTON

Ukhahlamba-Drakensberg, Lesotho, September 2001

Born of volcanic rock
the black hills undulate at the horizon.

At each outcropping
rock people emerge
from the depths of the mountain.

Ahead, the twelve apostles wait.
We ascend the twisted dirt path
to the place where the air is thin.

Like Lot's wife IIdeth
looking back has consequences
though not as final as hers.

Mud houses stand nearby.
Dark roofs pale walls:
The land of the San people.

Talk of the Bosoto
how they came to this land

Not like the Zulu, the white
recovering mercenary
turned tour guide says,
They breed and breed and breed …

She keeps things so shiny and clean
the South Asian woman from London whispers.
How long has she been married?

She, speaks English
but no one speaks to her.
Children and mothers
stand beside their houses
waiting for the gifts the visitors
bring in odd exchange for looking inside.

A young bony boy plucks
the 3 strings of his homemade guitar.
A sleepy drone for his long away father
rising in the dusty air.
Lonely eyes ask for something.

No school for the children.
Mothers have no money unless
their husbands go to South Africa
in search of the brilliant stone—
many never return.

Ambrose Smart

15 January 1827   Cape Negro, Purgatory Point

I

He did not know I want to kill him. Hannah know.
She took my knife from its secret pocket in my boot.

I fix my left hand tight round his throat.
I reach for my blade—it gone.
His sons jump me from behind knock me down.
He cough and sware, sware and cough: he say
Hannah is my property you hear, mine …
I spit in his red pock-mark face.

Hang me now or sell me. None of you safe
as long as God give me breath.

II

Hannah's hands could no longer caress him with desire.
Sometime Ambrose paid for more nimble ones
showing no signs of age or despair.

III

At Cape Negro, north east of Port La Tour,
the voice of the sea was strong that night.
Raging, raging until dawn when the fog arrived
to choke off the sunrise   smothering her
like the soft wool blanket her grandmother
spun before her birth.

Hannah couldn't see the ocean but felt its pull
especially on long summer days after the solstice

and before come the full moon.

IV

And I alone have escaped to tell you.

ADDENA SUMTER-FREITAG

Parked on Columbia and Main
Waiting for April to Get off Work

Letters: BA and ROMIO
graf-fit-erized themselves on the doors of the Pawn Shop across the street

along side the strange squiggles and arrows
and chicken-hawk symbols
That covered the walls beside them.

Woman number one floated by
(Which in itself seems odd that I chose that word
Because it contradicted her "Cracked-out-gait"
Yet somehow ... she seemed to float by)

The trumpety-thump-thump
Of her thighs
Clashing together (like huge cymbals)
As they rubbed balls of lint over their thunderous path
Alerted me to Woman #2 (who passed on the sidewalk)
"The storm" calmed as it traveled down her pant legs
And her feet seem to barely hit the ground
Before her legs Cannon-balled themselves into her next stride

Women number one, actually crossed in front of the car at an angle
On my "blind side"
My first glimpse of her (looking right into my eyes)
Sent a ripple of fright though-out me
And an impulse to lock the car door
came instinctively

But I knew she was watching me
And I was embarrassed ... somehow
that she might know
That a woman could frighten another woman

And it pained me!
And I cursed the times we live in
And **she** began to curse suddenly.
Maybe at me
Maybe the times

And **I** cursed again "in chorus"
Cause I thought it strange
That I would cast a critical eye
Upon my sistah's thighs

my, my
my, my
my, my, my!

ANTHONY JOYETTE

Reflections
For Samantha

Yesterday, stale heat
and frigid cold.
Simmered and preserved me,
a delicacy of this land.
For years, the humid feel
of nature's breath
sautéed my immigrant
sense of self,
to Canadian cuisine.
Like cold cuts and Poutine
I am no longer an
exotic dish of this or that,
but everything they are.
Cold humour and warm wishes,
Fashioned by the arms of diversity.
   More they, than what I used to be.

ADEBE DERANGO-ADEM

Terra Incognita

unchartered seas/skins unknown
histories/sins
regions unmapped
bodies undocumented
do not search for us in the ancient texts
or paraphernalia, we are *terres inconnues*,
have always been a people
to be discontinued

our body parts unknown,
thrown down to the *mare incognitum*,
we make our way to the remote corners
of the cosmos, worlds reserved
for the other, redraw maps
though we do not want to be fully explored

want only to be remembered
instead of forced to enter the realm of incognito
gnosis, the realm of knowledge
that is merely teaching cognizance
of difference

of *terra pericolosa*,
of blackness, the trans-Atlantic sea sickness
when our ghosts left Rome,
or the Pythagorean gore that preceded
our haunting and our lives
    the middle passage where I was born

and returned to *Kanata* where once upon a time
maps like skin meant nothing:

the endangered species in all of us, the mystery
not degradable, the Spirit
never sharp.

Marron Inconnu

the sea gives me elemental warnings as I wait
for signs of promise, signs
of solitudes being broken down and
bodies growing by tremor into new birth

into a moment when our native land
stretches its arms and I become we
for are we all not somehow abandoned in spirit
which is how the sea compensates
for our chaos of forms
      for are we not all awaiting judgment
which will test how we can keep still
and guarded against the storm of memory
that blurs our bodies against the winds
submerging the cliffs, the histories
books escaped:
blanc, mulatto, negre, marronage

our histories, songs of calypso
thrown into apocalypse

ADRIAN WORRELL

scenes from a winter home

78
it bursts
from frozen
tombs

even stars
shiver.

triple soul's furnace
testifies steamy
opaque.

breath is dragon's work

life's a screaming
revolt against an
insinuating
awake

canadian ash
coats my words.

81
bargain harold snowsuits
and
lost 'n found mittens.

we're little mattieu dacosta
motherfuckers
corpo fechado-like
breaking virgin
planes of inter-galactic
white and elder envy.

84

cardboard anointed with
"megaforce" polish or
the fish-cake grease
trapping friday night uncles'
home-slaking
six-love sketches

we pack
berice-calcutta-hk-accra-style,
scarborough style, banno.

and slide down the
time glazed child's mind
mountains

down
the killer's hill.

we slice between
knobby wrists
blooming grotesque
airy grasps mock
blazing blinding
nothing with:
"the spring will see me green
… know that the spring will!"

down
the hill.

we land on argentine

daring krik? krak?
gut rumbles of
sleep-water waking

krik
krik
krak

memory's alchemy:
gossip and worry
would immortalize
survivors
in hissing bronzes
of hero and of coward.

krik

muted panic
hushes even silence

to the argentine host
we pour libation stillness.

krak
krak.

wayside jason laughs
scared then prays sweat.

ginger steps spirit
us to quiet ground.

we say nothing
this time scaling
killer hill.

"this time jason's driving"
everyone laughs.

stars creep closer
as if to watch.

86
a snap shot
beats danny chung's
glove hand
cory
his mouth ringed
with patty flakes and
freeze dried hork
pisses on to white.

"danny" he says, cupping his topaz sludge
"you want an apple juice snow cone?"

87
the shovel's
a catfish's mouth

beaded asphalt
hosts work like
triangle trade deep
sea dredging

and i
for stolen moments
am

granddad, great granddad
grandma, great grandma

wukking de groung
up in de groung
wukking de groung.

"you! plantation land selling off!"

"uncle, sennup a piece of
yam or pumpkin
from de groung
eddoes
from de groung"

i say
and
dive into my
crumbled
pyramid.

90

a xxx fat goose
five-finger
discount accomplice.
bearing 12 inches dax, and macy's
dowry.

from stc to kennedy
fraternal danger
eyes me

i pull my hat low and
feel for my blade

93

flame or turbo?
berner trail or featherstone?
ol' patra and new buju.

bubbling
her black
on my beige.

leaving

.38 slugs
shriek their doppler
ascension

a body falls
full of creeping cold

cory's laughing,
"fuck it, star. jail?
it fall from the sky here, star."

dead heat cools
engine block hot

brain white get-a-way cars
trade of kilo/meters
and practiced spite

"see it deh? it's all 'bout.
falling from the fucking sky."

we walk
warm and easy
as if
cool and deadly

walking to where
we chained
our bikes

98
it pounces all eager-like
teasing breath with ice
asthma; exciting thots of
turning back

home.

"yo, differently, back home,
make it rain too hard
they ain't leaving their gates, guy."
i hear cory say
"them really don't know nothing 'bout cold."

they don't know.
back home
about these
routes.

BERTRAND BICKERSTETH

I Look At My Hand

I look at my hand and I see the prairies rolling up
against the Rockies,
elephantine grooves rippling like unknowable coulees,
undulant and unnamed, across my skin,
a dusting of snow fallen ash scattered along the membrane
    between fingers,
deep and dark as loam.

Make no mistake, when your sky cracks open with a sudden thunder
it is my snap!

We, Too

We, too, sing Alberta, from the first jail in Calgary and the wronged
    belonging of this familiar place.

We, too, sing of Cyclone the Big Black Buck, too, sing for Cyclone,
    sing like Cyclone the Big Black Buck,
                              the eternal
    Northern Star of the greatest outdoor show on earth.

We, too, wail in these Northlands this side of la rivière de la paix
Oui, tu peux chanter, il te *faut* chanter ici aussi.

This *faux* was not our fault, this dislocated Harlem farming, just
    north of Athabasca: You
        called/We responded
        All right, all right, now we are OK here, too (and KS, MS,
MO and, OH, even IL, here, too).

And we, too, sing Alberta
the Babylon psalm rounded up along

the erupted rockies, one renamed ridge, and
the evaporating elevated grain

the faded stain of segregated schools
the suppressed success of our homes

steaded in the prairie bush
the land, its hues

the language we hews
the semple blues of Hughes

with the grinning dues of Ware
granted by MacEwan, our prairie uncle.

Too, the bellows in the bowels of the overground
railroad, we sing, portered and pulled, man,

prairied by night
moonstruck by the days

of a Chinook shine
at the hill's foot

shuffling to the pulse of black blood
we were babies born in tar

sands but we're not from here
sing the refrain: where are you from?

You know dis beat dis rupture may sound wrong

                                                     to you

but we, too, sing this strange Alberta song.

CHARLES C. SMITH

paradox
(for charlie parker and martin luther king, jr.)

in the final moment   it's what we learn from the body
how it is seen   atop a sterile chrome table
covered in white cloth   the blood
now stuck   in the breath

whether the mouth   was a sax or microphone
it wore out   all their stress

and became   an addiction
with the openness   of moon light
pushing in   on their dark brown foreheads

it was then   they were held
to god truth   and white powder
their full weight   lying inert

some doctor poked each   with a tube
said   "looks like

someone   in his sixties"
even tho they both beat this by more than twenty years

this is what it ate of them   the hate and bitterness
envy and long solitudes   a penetrating sight

showed in their lungs   scarred tissue
along the heart's wall   gave sign they had lived

beyond the time   any might suspect
from their birth   certificates

34 and 39   and what remains to tell in their absence

they each defined   what the world could only show them
violence at first instance

clinging like sorrow
their nostrils   clogged with pain

birchtown in flames

just outside shelbourne   july 1784
an "extraordinary mob   or riot"

unemployed disbanded soldiers   with guns
found their way   to the other side

drowning churches and houses   with torches
herding men and women   children and dogs

and leaving some   sucking stones
the skies full of clouds   smoke and stars

caves became sepulchers   without light
and blood ran into roots   like a downpour

so that the wooded   roads rushed red
between   these two towns

one full of transactions   like a crescent
moon bartering   with night

the other caught up   like a snake in a garter
all of its venom   squeezed out at the teeth

one built on white lace   foodstuffs and rum
anchoring boats   from the stretches of an early empire

the other veiled in emptiness   taking each day
like a prayer   and trading all they had

both slammed hammers   into this port city
while others   gambled the differences

between those who worked   and what they were paid
by the official surveyor   who too faced weapons

that were suddenly unconcealed

until the army   sat in a warship in the harbour
and birchtown   lay like a corpse decomposing in an open field

then the tally   in stock and bodies
all assets liabilities fatalities   the tabulations seemingly endless

claims and counters in courtrooms   the early
jurisprudence of this state   and as always

after recording   property and labour
there was no time given   for other stories

JOY RUSSELL

ABC Passage

Crossing X,
anonymous name,
Legba[1] to get you over.

Trickster marks
the spot, black & frisked
& ready to rock,

roll, rewind,
what left behind,
what's up

ahead. X in silence,
two lines crisscross.
Double trouble, double bubble.

Bubbly blind, bubbly bad.
Crossing X to get to Z,
just to start all over

on A. We'll spin
cycle the sea, dry that
hambone been around

& back again; drift ashore
on our own flotsam & jetsam
—send a message in a bottle.

Crossing X, the treasure hunt,
booty bounty bling bling.
Pirates & profiteers working

the alphabet to forget our names
—you know, it's so low
you can't get around it,

so high, you can't get—
The signature tune: Razzle Dazzle
& Muzzle. Now Trickster's got them

by the long nose, all those fabrications
for the Emperor's clothes. A complicit
crowd—fools bamboozled, vocal

chords unsaying. We earth-land,
SOS stories in sand, every grain
literate, each grain record.

MICHAEL FRASER

Underground

They came like caged birds
railed out in bottoms
of sunken wood crates,
their nostrils pickled
in sour stench coats,
summer's humid claws
baked them weak
as crickets squeaked wings
under slow moving stars

even near the border,
they were always one cough
away from the familiar
clinking chain bracelet,
the scalding half-tone whip
boiling bumps onto their backs
like a firebrand fresh from
blue hot fire

and when they crossed over
into Ontario,
the photograph showed it all,
Africans knee deep
in a vomit of snow
a halloween of lies
while they listened
to the frozen icicle notes
crash one by one
in the icestorm's wake,
the strangled crunch of boots
waiting for the full husk of winter
to burst open

and in spring
they didn't know what to expect
with the new crops and all,
and when they dreamed of cotton
their screams shucked the night air
of its clothes
and their hearts raced
alongside the cold curdling voices
running barefoot into morning.

SHAUNTAY GRANT

untitled

i remember her
coming home
from the grave
to cure the rain

she was a touch
of wind
in my throat
stirrin up shit
that bound us up
for teaching

stubborn and frigid
we were
pellets
warring and clumped
holding hard to form 'til
she let go the ghost
switched-whipped our lips
then tender

listen

and our pride
put our backs
to the rain

grandmother

take my hands
and make them
magic

i want to know
the labour
of knuckles
cracked and
calloused
worn from washboards
weaving birch bark
and parable

merge memories
like hair follicles
cornrow stiff
scratch the scalp
of my subconscious
grandmother
teach me

cover me patches
heaps of ragged cloth
soiled bleak with berry
shrubs and gutter muck

brew me a root tea
back-bush and potent
cure colds and
drive-out freeze
with goose fat and
other
questionable fixes
foul-smelling
greased and rotten
healing
mending

teach me avoid
light signposts
for bear tracks
and hunter

show me secret
ways of feeding
from forest feasts
flour dumplings and
blueberry stew i want
to know
potatoes
pan fried
pain
too much
on the belly
grandmother
teach me

sing me songs to summon
dreams
and charm a child
towards sleeping

fix firm your roots to cover
crowd my home
grandmother
teach me
teach me
teach me from your life–giving bones

Obfuscations of Academia

When it comes to democracy,
pursuit of the good life, making money,
subjects and verbs aren't expected to agree,
free enterprise is trumpeted,
free speech is holy,
like eloquence,
education is celebrated, applauded,
given leadership, economic development roles.

Prosperity: power of affordability, indulgence,
culture of youthfulness, sexuality,
engendering casualness to the seriousness,
complexities, demands of responsible parenting,
educational amnesia—
forgetfulness as to its transformative power,
investing in their child's future.

Abrogation of responsibility—
ignoring oppositional attitudes, bad behaviour,
laxity ensuring assignments, study gets done
have children not interested in learning,
underperforming, failing, dropping out,
disconnected, dismissive to society's mores,
schools charged for parental failures.

Educational institutions
confused about their raison d'être, failing
to demand higher standards from faculty,
uphold academic excellence, teaching accountability,
release those who have lost their passion,
invest in teacher re-education programs,
inspire, raise students' educational aspirations,
unleashing mobs, gangs, populations,
unable to advance themselves, society.

RUDYARD FEARON

I Thirst

I thirst
for the desert
that flourishes
in Luther's soul;
the winter-worn tree
that roots in
long gone spring.

I thirst
for the dusty sea
that awaits
in its nakedness
the corpse
of my mind.

Lost Tongue

I must break
this language
so that I may speak ….

WAYNE SALMON

Curriculum

I must speak bi-lingual
Neither one of them mine ….

I must study centuries of history
None of it mine ….

I read a thousand voices
None of them speak to me
Not one of them speak of me

Am I entirely obscure?

I see you Talk 'n Teach
But I can't hear a word you say.

WHITNEY FRENCH

a wish

the language i speak in is hollow and black
words hang loose from the ends of a tree
to form a sentence, a lettering mosaic
prosaic sensations spark a fire
across the wordy forest, resistant to steel
ablaze a ways away from the domestic

handsome houses sparkle of domestic
dialect, convoluted context in white and black
newsprint, vowels volley against lamppost steel
consonants swish in sewers, no tree
speaks freely just barred in parks, fire
trapped in a lighter-candle-light-bulb mosaic

pieces of wood and glass will smash in mosaic
prophecy, the words wrapped in the domestic
glossary separating the oxygen from fire
leaving behind a carbon copy, smudging black
prints, scars and bruises and gashes on trees
until we stand in the shade of steel

birds etch symbols on branches of steel
word choices sparkle how a coloured mosaic
reflects like a window to let go a lingo, a tree
trunk's terminology turns domestic
a translation from beats to beeps, from black
to streetlights, our cellphones' glow replaces fire.

the language i speak spits fire
from the tongue, stories tougher than steel
sealing secrets from centuries of darkness and black
our resources broken but pieced together a mosaic
of natural manufactual evidences of the domestic
packaged Mother Nature's tongue from the skin of a tree

plant a word like a seed in hopes that a tree
will take root and spread like a fire
bridging the language of the natural and domestic
unifying branches and steel
together, broken horizons trace a mosaic
rainbow that flashes for a moment, then folds into black

into something so black that it darkens in the shadow of a tree
and while under the mosaic of light—the leaves, pieces of fire,
i declare my opponent: steel, my enemy: all things domestic.

PAMELA "PAM" MORDECAI

Temitope

> *temitope:* Yoruba word for "enough to give thanks" or "give thanks to God!" A name for both males and females, though more often females.
> *igba:* Yoruba word with many meanings including rope, two hundred, time/season, garden egg
> *Olorun*: Creator, Supreme Being, one of many names for the Yoruba Sky God

My daughter tells me, "Mum, I don't have much
more time, so I do not intend to read
hundreds of baby books." She's thirty-eight.
The girl child she is carrying is her first.
I tell her, "Love, it isn't very kind
of you to tell someone who's sixty-four
about not having much more time!"
But it is really fine. We say it is
longer than rope, this time, this word that has
no synonym, being itself or not
itself, being, rather, liminal, an interstice
between just then and a moment about
to be. But we who come from islands know,
crac-cric, periphrastic, is so life go.

And as for baby books, we never read
not one. We birthed you, named you, kept you clean,
fed you, sent you to school, prayed God you would
come to no harm. That cord of hours played out
by tiefing hands so long ago to snare you on your way
back home, full bucket on your head, humming
as your swift feet spat sand, slant eyes smiled at
the spinning wheel of huts ahead, ears shut
against the loud demanding threads of smoke
from their cook fires: "Sapling, how come we wait
the whole day and you don't reach home?" And then,
"How come you fade like mist and nobody see you again?"

How could we know a coffle choked your song
air buckled in your throat as you grew thin

down a rat's hole dug deep in watery dirt?
How could we know they flayed your bark with whips
rammed you between felled trees trussed end to end
seasoned in vomit, blood and shit? Our tears
spilled from closed eyes scoured pots of memory
as fitful slumber tossed our heads, tumbled our dreams.
We sought to conjure labyrinths crisscrossed
by footprints shouting still, "Time you reach home!"
We counted cowries hours, weeks, centuries.
We prayed, day-clean and dark, "Olorun grant
the stolen ones igba, a rope to climb
out of fate's pit to eat sweet dates again,
to see through green lashes of leaves your home of sky."
Olorun heard. The infant came on a red string. Temitope.

SEBLE SAMUEL

Intention

creating communities with sand
stacking sand castles with young hands
and sharing potlucks with acquaintances
for so long till you can't remember when
sand no longer slipped through fingers
because the pebbles together
became unwavering rocks of support
and these acquaintances became love
a love as profound as family
so that their deaths carved out
gaping holes in our personal histories

stolen breaths
and an aching for those
whose presence is deliberate
rehearsed deaths
and a narrow mindedness that
clouded humanity by institutions
only to realize our commonality
and our fragile state of vulnerability

if anything should happen, i'm right here

chosen families, and intention.

Greener Grasses

and here I thought
I was Canadian.
poorly built for this weather.
I need heat and sun
the doctor said.
diagnosed at age 7 with
Sickle Cell Anemia; a mutation of malaria
affecting those from tropical climates,
making me immune to malaria.
a lot of good this does me here in Canada.
perhaps in 100 years of global warming
if all the pine trees
are killed by pine beetles
and instead of planting pine trees
they plant palm trees
and Vancouver is pushed further inland
and the tropical insects find a new home
then maybe I'll finally be
built
for this weather.

BLOSSOM THOM

Free

I feel free.
I don't know my history
which is a good thing
because if I did, I might have to kill somebody
and that somebody might be me.

They complain as they reign on this piece of dirt
as if it were given to them by God
damn it we all know that's not true.
And I sit and consider what I can do to shut them up
which is really quite clever
being so boring that a lady would consider whoring for a moment of
    peace.

But that's a slave mentality.
Grounded in generations of striving and never arriving
Praying, hoping, barely coping

I am free.
And it's time that you learned to contend with me
on my terms.

If you insist that I should have a dream
I will remind you that I am wide awake
and ready to break your ass.
But I won't.
Because I'm a pacifist.

Don't suggest that
any little success
is dependent on leaving behind my clothes, my hair, the rest.

If you clear that muck from your mouth, your ears, and your eyes
you would realize
that they who pray, hope, and barely cope
are not those who will overcome.
Like me, they are sentinels to what was, what is, and what will be.
Our lineage runs from antiquity to infinity.

Kings, queens, the rabble, and the rude
Your blessings are true.
Our prayer, this poem, is for you.

MARVA JACKSON LORD

mo ving

jamaica
i remember a room full of sun mom dad voices
a veranda looking out onto a street a woman walking towards me with
something in her hands
i remember sitting in a bus in my crinoline dress

another veranda covered in fine fern leaves
part of a compound in Kingston
we share with at least one other person
i remember calling her auntie
i remember someone putting my brother to stand on top of a red ant's hill
the healing cactus tall in the garden to my young eyes
my brother and sister loud playing happy
coconut tree
ackee tree
my mother was beautiful and she had another child, a new sister
the hot coals of the fire which inspired my nickname "boon boon"
i remember chalk on the doors to keep out duppies [1]
dark nights

somewhere in the middle i remember saying goodbye to my father's
  mother
somewhere in the country
i remember her pale skin i remember i loved her very much

somewhere in the middle i remember my mother's mother with us in the
compound, standing near the chicken coops
she was so dark i remember i loved her very much

somewhere in the middle i remember cold mountain air and a beautiful
horizon

somewhere in the middle i remember the waves rushing in to shore
confusion about the swimming pool by the beach (the explanation
confused me too)

i remember white pink red flamingos and starting school in my blue
school uniform and
being happy and that i had a friend

canada
i remember when i was 4 flying on a plane to my new home
cold dark
plastic toy planes
airplane food lots of it
driving in a car
seeing the "indian" head on the tv screen
late night tiredness arriving in small sleeping town
happy but mom and dad often fighting, arguing, tension in the house
unhappiness

at least in jamaica it was warm

QUEENIE

Yellowknifed

When it was a mere 20 below, i'd think,
"Boy this is a great day, I can push back
my parka hood." I was used to New York winters,
this was nothing. 1953, Yellowknife,
in love with Beatrice Gonzales.
Followed her home to her native Canada.

Found work in a government office typing pool.
Some of us slept on the floor
when it was too cold to go home.
We'd fall asleep exchanging stories of our past.
Some women made it clear to me
my type of life was quite foreign.
They had absolutely no interest in me.

I made it clear I was not desperate.
That would be foolish.
Beatrice was a professional woman
of good standing, Vice Principal.
I was content with my comfortable life.

Now, you see, had I been a man, I could have got away
with touching a woman's cleavage, lifting
her petticoat up, even rubbing against her genitals.
If the woman tried to press charges,
she would be told she had encouraged it.
Asked what was she doing alone in a room,
with a man who wasn't her husband?
Told she must have made advances.

An attempted kiss would have been considered
trifling. Nothing to write home about.

Headlines read: "First Same-Sex Lesbian Case".
Branded a freak of nature.
The public need to be protected.
Yellow Knives were out to get me.

Gross indecency was my crime.
Nobody asked me any questions.
Guilty on a white woman's evidence alone.

In court Laura claimed that she looked up at me
from her desk. I was supposed
to have looked strangely at her,
a rather concentrated look.
She claimed to look down. She said
I grabbed hold of her, tried to kiss her.
As she pushed me away,
I was to have said "You're very cruel," and she
began to cry.

Of course I looked at her, even undressed her with my eyes,
And she undressed me too.
"Exotic" she whispered,
in the next breath spat out: "You beast."
She locked eyes with me,
our lips brushed and she cried,
"No stop! I can't. I'm not strange like you."

I was the first woman arrested and tried
in a Canadian court, gross indecency
against another woman. I was
Yellowknifed.
I was Black.
Guilt?

This poem is based on the first same-sex lesbian assault criminal case to be tried in a Canadian court. In 1955 a white woman "Laura" (pseudonym used to protect her identity) took Willimae Moore, an African American woman, to court for gross indecency, in Yellowknife, Northwest Territories. Ms Moore was found guilty. She and her white Canadian lover, Beatrice Gonzales, were hounded out of the town. Even though she subsequently appealed the decision and won, her name was tarnished forever.

ZAKIYA TOBY

Another Land Between 4 Brick Walls

Calypso vibes and reggae chunes linger in my mind
Subtle reminders of a land I claim as home
Even if only for a vacation

My foot does tap to a different beat
Somehow I cyah stay still when the music hits me
Trini to di bone while waving a maple lined flag

Having two cultures flowing through my veins
Makes me incredibly well balanced
I knew not to push the boundary too far
Because different were my consequences

My parents wouldn't let me be just a normal Canadian kid
No sleep overs or talking back or from some serious licks I hid
"Yuh betta be home before di lights come on
Or else crapaud¹ smoke your pipe!"

With threats like that I had no other choice
But to straighten up and fly right!

Broughtupsy? I had plenty
And manners enough for two
But sometimes I wanted to do
The things that normal kids do

I was the only one who took roast bake to school
And thought it was a treat
Complete with guava jam
Or some saltfish … mmm … nothing it could beat

No lack of roti shells
Or curry smells wafting through the house
Macaroni pie, stew chicken and pelau
Were the meals that watered my mouth!

It's a funny place to be living in another land between 4 brick walls
My friends never understood why I said "channa"
Or why we put Angostura in di orange juice
Why I called dishes "wares"
Or why I would sing "Di Parang Now Start"
Instead of Frosty the Snowman
But they loved me just the same

It's not always easy trying to balance the old with the new
Finding that very fine line in the sand
But my parents somehow managed to do the best they could
In this new home country land

I have memories of my mother
dragging herself across ice in sneakers
Trying to help me learn to skate
Or speaking her best version of français
To help me make a grade

All the lessons I wanted, I had
Swimming lessons were a must
Add ice skating, piano and violin
At the time I didn't understand the fuss

I was propelled through stereotypes
Of "Blacks can't do this or that"
Because my parents accomplished great things
Beautiful educated people in my home who
I had the honour of witnessing

I will never be just a normal kid
But I'm Canadian just the same

Somehow a little piece of my heart is still tabanca
For my home land far away

… Sweet sweet TnT, oh how I love up dis country …

HAROLD HEAD

Resume

NAME:	Man
SOCIAL SECURITY:	None
ADDRESS:	Journey to Freedom
EDUCATION:	University of the Streets
PAST EMPLOYMENT:	Participated in the Liberation of
	Algeria
	The Congo
	Kenya
	Cuba
	Vietnam
POSITION DESIRED:	Restoration of Dignity
	& Respect of the Indian Nations
	Bantustan in Babylon

REFERENCES:	Ahmed ben Bella
	Patrice Lumumba
	Jomo Kenyatta
	Che Guevara
	Ho Chi Minh
ORGANISATIONS:	Associated with
	the oppressed
	peoples of the world
MINIMUM SALARY REQUIREMENT:	Liberación

STAGE

Dub

Based on interviews by Valerie Mason-John
with Klyde Broox and Lillian Allen

What is Dubpoetry?

Author and internationally renowned Canadian dub poet Klyde
Broox turns the question around: "Dubpoetry what is?" He adds:
"It is the rearranging and shifting of words to create new meanings
and new ideas." Dubpoetry is one word said in one breath. There
is no gap between the dub and the poetry or between the words
and the poet.

Lillian Allen, one of the founding mothers of Dubpoetry in Canada,
says: "Dubpoetry goes to the heart. The heart of the matter. The word.
It's a form that emerges out of the people, their utterances, their need
for voice, articulating their experience, their ideas, their visionary
fervor, and aesthetic beauty."

Dubpoetry is often described as emerging from a cross-pollination of
reggae music beats and spoken word. However, the Eurocentric poetry
establishment and white Western academics have simplified it as
"protest" poetry, not understanding the complexities of African oral
and scribal traditions. Dubpoetry exists for both the stage and the
page. In fact you might say that the poet's page *is* the stage. When
reading dubpoetry, we must be able to hear the phonetics of the
vernacular sing in our ears, speak from the page.

Allen says: "Dubpoetry was originally based on our political activism.
It was an art form meant to do political work. Dub took it cues from
Reggae, and Reggae took it cues from Louise Bennett who took her
cues from the way Jamaican people expressed themselves. She
empowered a language from the beauty of everyday talk, and was
responsible for Jamaican Patois being recognized as a national language
in Jamaica, and of course, something to be proud of."

Broox speaks of dubpoetry as the "edge of the coin." "Every coin has
three sides. There is the oral on one side and the scribal on the other,
and dubpoetry resides at the edge, providing a bridge."

Dub culture existed long before dubpoetry, he says. "It was the words
in motion from the preacher, the market woman, the hawker, the

storyteller. Dubpoetry is the resurgence of the Griot and the Jali traditions of Africa blended with the English traditions." Allen reiterates that: "Dub poets take everyday speech and stylize it into an artistic form with rhythm, and heave and sway of the heart beat. Dub inscribes resistance as well as pain, and passage as well as joy. A sense of personal and collective empowerment drives dub's possibilities. The intention of dub poetry is to disrupt traditional discourse, to call attention to fullness and wholeness of life that has been ignored. Dub lifts the people up."

The name was coined in the 1970s by Linton Kwesi Johnson and Oku Onoru, who write in their book *Echoes* that dubpoetry is "the laugher/cry/sigh/sign of the people."

In Canada, dubpoetry has developed as a strong Black voice heard both nationally and internationally. Lillian Allen, Afua Cooper and Ahdri Zhina Mandiela were among the founding mothers of this genre in Canada during the 1980s. Allen (who has won two Juno awards) was particularly pivotal; she and Jean Binta Breeze (in the UK) were two of the first women to introduce the female voice and female issues to the dub register. Until then dub had been male-driven in Jamaica and the UK.

In 2003 Allen set up the Dub Poets Collective in Toronto. It can be argued that because of Lillian Allen, Toronto has the largest concentration of dub poets in the world outside of Jamaica. Newer Canadian poets like d'bi.young anitafrika are part of the lineage founded by Allen who are keeping the Jamaican culture alive in Canada. Young migrated from Jamaica to Canada in 1993, and ten years later was named by Toronto's **Now** Magazine as "best dub poet" and storytelling actor. She has won several awards, produced several dub albums, and has had several documentaries made about her work.

Broox credits Allen with having a great influence on his own style. "Dubpoetry can often be very heavy in tone," he says. "Lillian Allen allowed me to have a lighter voice." He also believes that dubpoetry is giving authority to Black Canadians internationally. "Dubpoetry is in the process of creating a Canadian Reggae."

"The mystique of dub is Black. It is Black anger, Black energy, repatriation. But anyone can do dubpoetry because it is reclaiming one's own vernacular," says Broox. "It is the use of body, language, rhythm, reverb and echo. Dubpoetry is a moistening word, an engineering word, a filming word. All the meanings of dub in the dictionary apply to dub poetry. Dub poets make the people the subject and historicize the daily life. Dub poems are not ornaments to be reflected upon, but instruments to make music with."

LILLIAN ALLEN

Black Voice Can't Hide

A voice signifies the real, relational
                    spirit thought quest

model dependent breath
A shadow's feel, noh soh real
apparition imagination digital
Virtual & reality and virtual reality
Physics' dualities
Beyond conventions to reinventions

A voice becomes when it stands
                    when it stands for something

Questioning and voicing to feel
                    a sense of the real
Poets turning routine into rituals
resounding sound symbols of language
                    into language play
un-ravelling the perfect embroidered geometry of the uni-lateral real
with its intricate layers of who, when, where and how to feel
The what shall speak for itself, the poet says
                    the poet says
The what shall be what the poet sees
Voice threading stance and eyes and light
pulled through the cracks in things that let the light in

An order against disorder and randomness expressed
in the poet's sound   voice sounding, re-sounding in the poet's
  sound

So to you the young poets who stand up
                              and voice
                                        crafted vision, sight-up into
    lines
set alight the energy in words, image, vibes
Say wey yu haffi say fi nuh buss' up, fi self-define, don't walk blind

(Mi sey) To you word chatterers, goes the glory
                                        a play forward link in our ancestor's
    story
word sound powa connectivity stations
spiritual underground railroad vibrations
                              self determination navigation
One voice, then two in community
                              ever exploring
a trikkle, then a clump, dem a movement worldwide

Oonu[1] own book vital ital alive with pride
Spoken word dub poetry vibe
Spoken word dub poetry vibe

Black Voice caan hide
Black voice can't hide

So there's Black Voice

Toronto – pOetic gEsture

An' de beat of Toronto
ah rhythm & sway
cannot wait to be embraced
This diverse alive in verse city
where trees grow around the cement
Our new self in concrete
Our feet against concrete
As we go about our ways
Percussion play echoing
learning to love what we have made
softening between brick and cement
a built-up world, steeples and stairs
glass mirrors
sparring for social change

New voices roasted enwrapped in ice
My mother walked from the plane into a fridge
That is Toronto in winter
"The best of times" she says "and the coldest of times"
Incubating a whirl of creativity
And visionary relativities
Ideas swirl, cultural voices unfurl
Making us larger than we are   becoming
Dub Poetry, Hip Hop, Opera,
Visual smarts and Community   Arts

Toronto in Excelsis!

You Toronto are my water bottle
My arts thirst quencher
No matter how far I roam
You pull me back
Your wide-open welcoming arms
A union formed
Our web of connection becomes visible
With every brush stroke on canvas
every stone carved
with every architect's vision
every note from the heart

An' for those who lived strident
and have gone before
Let their names not be forgotten
but be called who they truly are
Lovers of Justice, standing for peace, not war.

And to all the battles fought
Freedom sought on the grounds of Queen's Park
and Nathan Phillips Square, City Hall
or the roar of communities at Young and Bloor
"down with inequality, injustice, brutality"
International Women's Day parade, Caribana jump up
You have made our City strong
A republic of possibilities
A home to belong

We are trees standing in the water
A gathering of tribes
An abundance of hope
A destiny and a destination
from which a future must be forged
We were community before Simcoe
We are Hurons, and visitors and traders
Adventurers and underground railroaders
We are the Iroquois promise of unity
We are Kensington and Parkdale, Palmerston and Jane an' Finch
We're High Park and East York, Forest Hill and Yorkville
We're Rosedale and Cawthra Square, Regent Park and North York
We're Bloor Street and Junction, Harbourfront and Eglinton
We are a three million sided heart

And homelessness is us

Our little scar
That part split off
Lost, hiding, frightened, too tired to fight
Or resolved too soon
Needing a way back to the promise

Oh yes, we are the "superman" Joe Schuster penned to paper
An experiment splashed by the waves of Lake Ontario
prancing for a great makeover
The postmodern too slow a nation
It was no slam-dunk from Hubbard to Zanana

We are our parklands, winding creeks, nature preserves
We are free public spaces, ravines of lush graces
protected wetlands
We are the Humber and the Don

"fishing weir"

We are a thousand miles from our longings
Pinning dreams on over twenty thousand street corners
With many bridges to cross over
We are the beat, a city in heat
Alive, diverse and strutting verse
We are new age digital microwave
satellite communicators

We are our peoples' toil in this land
Our dreams alive in this land
A three million sided heart is this land
We are Toronto
          an experiment gone grand

For Diasporic Dialogue to commemorate Toronto's 145th anniversary.

KLYDE BROOX

NeoCanadian Version

Having often seen rousing
Screenings of the movie Cool Runnings
I know a bit about bobsledding
But I've never ever gone tobogganing
Although I'm not a newcomer to Canada
I am no eager-beaver tundra explorer
Yet, I'm sure that I am no longer a visitor

Don't like being seen as a permanent immigrant
Constant suspicion is an irritant
Makes one more vigilant than jubilant
More defiant than compliant
Don't label my skin color as deviant
Table my character as more relevant
It matters not where I'm from; in my heart I am
As much of a Canadian as any other one
From Toronto, Ontario, to Saskatoon, Saskatchewan
I am a Canadian patriot; neoCanadian patriot

Creole livalek, "nuff rispek"
Viva Quebec; although I can't parlay
Much in France, say, you
Can still hear me merci beacoup
To rendezvous over a beer or few
I might not be red, white, or Labatt Blue
And as you should know, "mi nuh name Joe"
But I can talk hockey too, although I don't love it
As much as you might do; however, I do
Admire the pleasures of the puck
Just like any born Canuck

I am happy to recall cultural adventures in Montreal
And sometimes I even get swept up into thinking
How cool it could be to go curling
Even going as far as to imagine
Gliding into speed or figureskating
Slipsliding by snowmobiling
Moving on up over mountains skiing

Splashing down rushing and rowing
Oohing and aahing into canoeing or kayaking
Growing flag of Canada-pride inside me unfurling
Engrafted maple leaf in my heart fervently fluttering
Never mind who wants me to merely mutter
I will proudly utter from atop the CN Tower!
Foreign accent or not; I am declaring dat
I am a Canadian patriot; neoCanadian patriot!

Sifting sagas of eras of Upper and lowered Canada
I share miseries and glories of past pioneer stories
Stories like Susanna Moodie's
She roughed it in the bush; shovel I come push
Indelible voices build bridges across ages
Voices like Louis the Riel, who was compelled to rebel
Voices that still will not forget to speak
Of horrors like the hanging of Angélique
Critique the mystique of a sneaky slavery

Apartheid template, Indigenous agonies
Assorted atrocities under carpet swept
Infested blankets, residential schools and
Ab-original lands stolen by power of pen
Self-destruction conditioned into generations
Struggles of reclamation for First Nations
No more rural or urban reservation
Abandon Canadian Bantustan!
Time to blend into one nation
To celebrate and not berate
Canada's open embrace of immigration

I arrived at the airport without a wintercoat
But with tongue to tell that I can count and spell
Underground Railroad did not always end well
Buxton, Africville, Jane and Finch!
People who feel it know the pinch
Nevertheless; regardless of all that and what is not
I am still a Canadian patriot, neoCanadian patriot

Nowhere near being a Pierre Elliot
Yet, I am becoming intimate with
Canada's indomitable spirit
I have inhaled the Northwind's breath
Mused among maple trees
Had my nose teased by Lake Erie's breeze
Weathered bonefreezing, bloodchilling winterwinds
Uttered angry litany of oldman winter's tyranny
Survived shrieking frostbitten nights which require fire
Liquour, and sharing soulwarming summerstories
Spicy, awesome autumn memories loudly painted
Multilayered, bundled up, snowed in, sheltering
Oftentimes, behind my eyes, I visualize
Spring sunrise awaiting winter's long, lingering demise
I will forever bless my beloved island of birth
But this monumental land is now my home on Earth
I am a Canadian patriot; neoCanadian patriot
Better to believe it than not

I probably won't manage to own a cottage
My written word may never earn me
A name as revered and acclaimed
As the award-winning Austin,
Or George Elliott, Clarke
Well known at Queen's Park

I might not write myself into wide Canadian attention
As resoundingly and profoundly as Lillian or Dionne
Not to mention earning a name as towering
As that of the great George Bowering

I don't envision parades of adoration
Nor entertain any delusion
Of perhaps ever being seen
To be half as good as Margaret Atwood
Maybe even a little as noteworthy
As the mighty Al Purdy

Or slightly as eminent a literary entity
As well distinguished and accomplished
As Michael Ondaatje
When first to this land I came
It seemed no-one knew my name
And maybe Canada will never fully know of me
Much less to blow my horn long after I'm gone
Like how I'm happy to mention Milton Acorn

Presences of blended essences
Narratives of neoCanadian identities
Tongue rooted in Africa
Seasoned in Jamaican Patwa flavor
Dipped in the wild waters of Niagara
My lips sip nuances of one hundred languages
Anointed by many voices my mouth speaks out
To tout a pathway to what could be called neoCanada Day
From the tip of the Rockies to the bottom of Hudson Bay

On my way to becoming neoCanadian
I have travelled the fabled Yukon
Where one cannot help but notice
It's still the stomping ground of Robert Service
And I've been hearing
Hints of a Canadian Reggae sound
Grounded in rugged rhythmic rocks of
Newfoundland

Always a pleasure to encounter
The charisma of Alberta
Especially Calgary, capital city of poetry

When first I went out West
My heart indeed was blessed
My eyes caressed, beholding
British Columbia's unfolding
Caribbeanesque contours

Border crossings spin nostalgia's vista
Eye-catching etchings as durable and valuable
As the White Spruce of Manitoba

Oh what grandeur, shining splendors!
South Western Ontario's soaring summers
Sunlit insights unveiled along Bruce Trail
I spy; irie islands in the sky, as I
Sail gracious gazes across my Hamilton Harbor

Pursuing poetry's whims and fancies
My itinerant eye fishes for rhymes
Parsing paradigms of the Maritimes
Aiming for figures of speech that span the
Massive expanse of Northumberland Strait
Then to quench my metric thirst, I often pluck verse
Out of the windcurrents of the Gulf of St. Lawrence

Poised between past and future tense
My pen extends itself to cast dubpoetic gestures
From Gulf of Alaska to Nova Scotia Peninsula
Pitch epic echoes all over the entire Arctic Archipelago
Alliterate its flow into the
Fine fluid folksiness of New Brunswick

I've eaten venison and veal
But not even tasted seal
All the things this poem wants to say
Could cover the TransCanada Highway
Craft an Atlantic-to-Pacific connecting
Lyrical line from Dawson City's downtown core
To the friendly shores of Labrador
I would love to dub a poem tour
From one shining sea to another

Overflowing cups of Canadian charm
Huddling and cuddling we keep warm
Drink daily, at least one Tim Horton's coffee
My specialty, mostly medium, steamy
Unsweetened, usually black like me
But every now and then I indulge in
Half-a-sugar with double cream
Stirring and sipping my neoCanadian dream
Convergent tributaries refresh mainstream

Being too old for backpacking; I love to go laptopping
Google tripping, online province hopping
Leisurely click-hiking pages of pensive prairie fields
My mind as firm and fertile as the Canadian Shield
I stand on guard as a bard in my adopted yard
Staring from Whitehorse to Prince Edward Island
With an eye to versify smiles of a thousand isles
As well as to amplify the hard to hear outcry
Struggle stories of the North West Territories

Much more than snow afoot in Nunavut
Sometimes seeming
As far from Canada as Lilliput
PanCanadian conversation
Sounds incomplete
Without soul of Inuit in it

Oh Canada, land of sign and wonder
Where paper ladder is also paper barrier
Here; migrant laborer becomes teacher
Immigrant teacher becomes laborer

Muralized mosaic
Pixels fixed in unequal space of place
Frozen; ache, for our true Canada
A culture-blender of a
Canada that belongs to all of us
Where justice, minus prejudice
Stands or falls for all of us
Thus duty to country
Stands tall in all of us

Then I can take the prize of a trip
I wish to make a grand overland Canada trek
Greeting daybreak on a bank of Great Bear Lake
Following my fancy up Mackenzie River
Fantasizing up myself
Shoulder to shoulder with Mt Nirvana
Uttering categorically, not metaphorically
I am a Canadian patriot, neoCanadian patriot!
Whether you want to scoff at, or lift your hat to that

CLAIRE HARRIS

MAri Performs

dear jass

dis is jes
to say
i fin' dis
in de out tray
an now sen'in
it to yuh

so cole
so mad an' baaad
like a stone trown

          enjoyin
            it own arc
              it shatterin
            contract
      wid glass

it brazen splintery
lannin

jes banal
to tink us aberashun
wha dere
to heal
in we variousness?
we who ent
flourish
ent metaphor

dis is jes'
to say
we is no
fragment so
we is we own
undah long
divishun
undah multiplicashun

sepahrate
as perfic' as
each floret
of de oleander
each keel
of hangin heliconia
as necessary
in we beautee
as necessary
as breat'

we so strange
we so entiah
is simple as honey
still fuh tea
we bloom
we strengt'
startle
yeah
leh we spit
on dis ordinary
doh we make it
togedder
yeah   us so spit

on integrashun
it swallow-up an'
buryin
leh we be
we own constellashun
a whole distric'
in orbit

is why we so
got to consent
bowin an'
kowtowin
to oblivion?

love

mAri

D'BI.YOUNG ANITAFRIKA

dis is a warning

jah9 tell dem seh dis is a warning
we nuh care weh yuh cum from
it's a new dawning
tell di people of di world revolushun's rising
look to di east and di west
it deh pon di horizon yes
tell yuh fren tell yuh moddah tell yuh cousin
we're a new generation we nuh fraida nuttin
we want we liberation from capitalist prison
don't call mi west indian
because I am an afrikan
dis is a warning a warning a warning a warning a warning
dis is a warning

misinformation dem a chat bout
filling di youts dem mind wid crabblehouse
education system waan rince out
a pure lie dem a tell tell tell
yuh guh to school 5 days of the week
relearning di fiction of his-story
written from di position of dem victory
but a pure lie dem a tell tell tell
suh won't yuh step inna mi class
and mek mi tell yuh bout di past
a new lesson for today
save the people of tomorrow

a time fi wi decolonize
oomaan and man seh we really really must realize
is a broken legacy we a legitimize
when we keep our eyes closed and act surprised
di likkle fellah pon di street
him a pack a likkle neat oozie
a ghetto yout wid few options
him seh gang a him family
watch him guh out in a blaze of glory
yuh membah when we used to play inna di dirt
and di bwoy dem used to lift up wi skirt
dandy-shandy hide and seek
spin di bokkle get a kiss pon di cheek and flirt
now yuh di youts dem a cum yuh haffi splirt
open up fire "everyone bite di dirt"
wid him big ole gun him wanna have fun
him don't know that him time soon cum

a time fi wi decapitalize
oomaan and man seh we must realize
a blood-bath legacy we a legitimize
when we keep our eyes closed and act surprised
likkle mary-sue seh she want blue eyes
ask her why and she started to cry
my cousin eileen get ice-cream
her skin's light-brown and pretty
yuh membah when we used to play dolly-house
you a di moddah me a di moddah
seh di shade a wi skin no it nevah mattah
well now mary-sue is 13
she's old enough to buy her own cream
ambi, nadinola, skin-lightener
seh she bleach out har skin suh she can be whiter
inna di futcha skin cancah
inna di futcha skin cancah
inna di futcha skin cancah

jah9 tell dem seh dis is a warning
we nuh care weh yuh cum from
it's a new dawning
tell di people of di world
revolushun's rising
look to di east and di west
it deh pon di horizon yes
tell yuh fren tell yuh moddah tell yuh cousin
we're a new generation we nuh fraida nuttin
we want we liberation from capitalist prison
don't call mi west indian
I am an afrikan
don't call west indian
i am born jamaican
don't call mi west indian
i am black womban
don't call mi west indian
i am from the moddah land
dis is a warning!
dis is a warning!
dis is a warning!
dis is a warning!

once upon a time
(to be sung in the tradition of gaelic ballads)

once upon a time today
in a land so far away
there lived a people deep as the earth
mother womb blessed their birth

the land gave food and love and hope
the land gave children to grow old
but soon the people grew restless with change
seek new lands they were told

the people walked and walked and walked
and walked and walked and walked and walked
to every corner and around
settling in new ground
many moons waxed and waned
many tides grew and died
many suns rose and set
yet the people did not forget

ase ase oya mother of nine
ase ase oya mother of wind
ase thunder lightning death and rebirth
ase our mother of change

then came the time of the warring ones
who killed their neighbours their sistahs their sons
from village to village they plundered and raped
forgetting oya's fate

they built great big birds of the seas
then packed their brothers and sisters beneath
then sold them one by two by three
how did this come to be

many more moons waxed and waned
many more tides grew and died
many more suns rose and set
and the people did forget

ase ase oya mother of nine
ase ase oya mother of wind
ase thunder lightning death and rebirth
ase our mother of change

come now my children of the night
wake you up from your slumbering sleep
our story calls with urgent flight
of how we came to be

across these oceans you must come
your sons and daughters have survived
five centuries beneath a divide

you are oya mother of nine
you are oya mother of wind
thunder lightning dead and rebirth
your name is oya
thunder lightning death and rebirth
your name is oya
thunder lightning death and rebirth
your name is change

ROBERT LAYNE A.K.A. MARKUS BLACK, THE ONLY GOOD NEGRO

Living Proof

It might be raggedy raggedy raggedy, but the yard will sweep
pon the cold ground not even a blanket
My brothers and my sisters them, they have to sleep,
They willing to drink
the water that you bath with, just to live
They never seen a doctor since they live, live, live
And if they reach the age of 5, it's graduation time
They become a refugee in their own country
One size fits all, you need no experience, zero tolerance
Don't you play ignorant
Let's take a look at this, if you will,
Let's see how much it took to get you in
It's not as bad as it looks, who is next of kin
Is my father's hand you shook, when you entering
Although the odds was set against you,
you came and walk a mile in my shoe
not just for the heck of it, it was father's wish
Now, wolf in sheep clothing, I can smell them for miles around
they been spook, they running like they mad
Taxi, taxi, I want to get away
take me to the mountains take me to the sea.

Fathers

Fathers, are they becoming an endangered species?

Dying on the street, trying to make 2 ends meet

What? Didn't you think I could handle myself on your block?

Always trying to put me on the spot, it only gives me a reason to use what
 I got

Now it's a little more than you bargained for

Turned atheist turned your back

Never say never when you know the streets full of terror

Now miss Dorothy sitting at home wondering why Tyrone is not coming
 home

But we all know why Tyrone is not coming home

Now left to moan is Thrones 2 sons him once disown

Trade your name in for a number, shackles on your hands and feet

I ain't going quietly and I am not accepting defeat

Mothers substituting for fathers while the children only taking orders
 echoing from the street

bosses

All waiting for another umbilical cord to be dropped

YVETTE DOUCETTE

proper english

I could
      write ah poem
wit me heart.

Why not 'ave a quill
dipped deep inside?
O what words would rise up wit de featha.

Praps dose me mout 'as not de dignity fuh.

De most tendah shoot
might rise up wit de featha
wrap itself 'round de shaft like growin tings do.
Rise up t'ward de light
come up fragrant like red earth just turnd
orange blossoms in early mornin
strong, crashin, me scented waves.

I could write ah poem
wit me heart's mysterious blood
from de blackness dere
I could write a poem while de pen turn 'n turn.

O what words would rise up wit de featha?

        Two wings flutterin,
        a small white bird caught
        in death's gray script,
          wings tremblin, foldin pon demselves.

Yes, praps de poem would say
what me mout hold tight between teeth.

I could write a poem
wit characters cut from feelin dese long days
dese fleetin, fleetin days

I could write ah poem wit me heart
de dark on de white page
dryin to Island-brown
de paper scented so of me inside.

Why not 'ave a quill pierce
what is again and again bruised and broken?
O what words would rise up wit de featha?

Praps de poem would say
what me mout 'as not de savagery to delivah.

De most tender shoot
might rise up with de featha,
wrap 'round de shaft like growin tings do,
rise up with de dark to writhe on de livin page
come up fragrant, fragrant
red earth just turnd
orange blossoms burst open
a great green wave, salt-laden.

I would write
wit me heart's mysterious blood
while de pen turn 'n turn
and de two white wings beat out
beat out freedom.

and love too

i search an hour fee ah poem ta send ta yuh
one dat could say dis 'bout your glance
how it slide like summer water
send silky ripples ta run cross my body
one dat puts down right
dat i see de deep true of yuh always
dat i feel it beatin' sa strong it warm me through

i search an hour fee ah poem ta send ta yuh
not one say dis love bloom like bayleaf bushes
tiny pink petahls against de winter stalks
nor one dat mention rain jewels in de hosta leaves
dat catch yer eyes bright an make yuh smile
no talk af de wind in pines, so lonesom sometime
none dat say dis love is stones becomin sand togeda

i search an hour fee ah poem ta send ta yuh
when i should be workin—damn, boy!
what poem could say how much i luv yuh low voice talkin
i fine no syllables strung togeda dat feel dis smooth
dis right, like de white inside af ah shell
what yuh brought me love cover my head 'gainst de dark
yuh is de poem dat me tongue like best de sound af

BROTHER SANKOFA

Blues on Jazz

An Ode To The Past, Present And Future …

I Was Feeling Restless & Blue … So I Went To Kemet On A
Spiritual Holi-day & Saw Billy
Picking Strange Fruits From Poplar Tree,
Roots Hanging From Putrid Earth … I Left Kemet & Went To Tibet,
And Met a Monk Name Thelonious … And We Spoke About
Melodious Sounds Of The
Mountains & About Free-ing Tibet … It Got Too Dangerous For
Me … So I Began Running …

I Was Running For Miles,
For My Free-Dome, When I Saw Mr. Davis From Miles.
So, I Said Mr. Davis I've Been Running For Miles Even Through
Muddy Waters For My
Freedom And Yet My Peoples Are Now Dumb & Free …

So, I decided To Travel Underground On The Rail Road … Then I
Jumped On The Train
From Kipling To Kennedy,
And Met John On The Trane,
And He Was Playin' With His Colt 45 On The Blue Train,
So, I Said "John Why U Playin' Wid Your Colt 45 On The Train?"
And He Replied, "Son This Is The Liberation Train—Come Ride
On This Colt Train, Come
Ride On This Blue Train, Get On The Liberation Trane."

And Suddenly, The Train Stopped And Shooked, I Felt Dizzy And
As My Eyes Cleared I
Saw My Good Friend Gillespie … Swaying In Back And
Forth … With Trumpet/Horns/Sax

I Got Off The Train And Went Up To Bathurst On Vaughn & Met
Up With Sa-Rah Lena On
Her Horns … Playin Sweet Jazz Symphonies …

You Can Hear The Scintillating Thudder Of The Sexophones,
On Your Ear Drums As It Take You On A Rhythmic Ride,
Bringing Orgasmic Highs and Low Blues.

This Is Jazz On Blues,
An Ode To All The Great Blues & Jazz Creators,
A Slice Of Jazz With Blues,
Season The Pot With Melodic Sounds Of Saxophonic & Trumphetic
Eclectic Vibrations.

I Come To Play Blues,
Erupting With Jazz Residues,
Staining Your Blue Sheets From The Intimate Rhapsodies Of Nina
& Simone … Singing U R
Young Gifted & Black … That's A Fact.

Her Smooth Velvety Voice,
Cries Of Melan-Choly Blues,
Bringing Hope Never Ending Joy.

Jazz On Blues,
Baked With Oppressed Souls,
The Pain, The Sorrow & Everlasting Hope … Still We Cope

Enslaved, But Not A Slave,
Go To Back Of The Bus, I Shall Not Be Moved,
Maafa, Snatch & Kidnapped, Middle Passage, Stolen & Raped
But Unbroken,

Plantations, Church Bombings, Lynchings—Crimes Against
Humanity, Doors Of No
Return,
Resisted, Fought
Revolution & Redemption …

I Had A Dream, Of Justice, Freedom And Equality,
So I Went To A Dinah In Washington,
To Speak With Dr. King On A Lonely Cole Nite,
To Discuss Strategies Of Liberating Peoples,
I Carried My BB In My Hand For Protection,
And King Told Me To Put It Away,
And I Complied And He Spoke About Non Violence & Turning The
Other Cheek … I Said Nat, And Turner Out Of The Dinah … And
Went Looking For Black Powa … In Mal-Colm
X … I Just Got Tired Of All These Injustices … So I went To Hear
Mo Betta Blues …

Blues Take Me To Bed At Nite,
And Jazz Wake Me Up In The Morning … Blues On Jazz …

ANITA STEWART

begging is a ting

begging is a ting a carry di swing
inna disya time it cyaan be a crime
begging is a ting a ting a carry di swing
inna disya time it cyaan be a crime

walk down town one a dem days
had to stand up a while and tek a good gaze
di city is plagued and it reach a stage
dat begging is a ting a carry di swing
inna disya time it cyaan be a crime
seh begging is a ting a ting a carry di swing
inna disya time it cyaan be a crime

madman a beg
seh him don't have no bread
the car-man answer
"you must be losing your head!
why i should take my money
give you sumting to eat?
find yourself a job and get off of the street"

"find myself a job and get off of the street?
if i could find myself a job
i would come off of the street!"

pickney deh a stoplight a wipe windscreen
dem seh beg yuh a ten cent mam, yuh nuh see di glass clean
di solushun to di problem by di war-crime police
fine di pickney dem and further force dem fi tief
lock dem inna jail, throw away di time
who give a damn if punishment nuh fit di crime

begging is a ting a carry di swing
inna disya time it cyaan be a crime
seh begging is a ting a ting a carry di swing
inna disya time it cyaan be a crime

riding on a bus, hear a womban a cuss
mi baby faada left mi wid ten pickney
suh mi last resort was to start start start
walking in di city and beg beg beg
hope dat mi get more than pity pity pity
hope that mi get some clothes pon mi back
and likkle food inna mi belly

begging is a ting a carry di swing
inna disya time it cyaan be a crime
seh begging is a ting a ting a carry di swing
inna disya time it cyaan be a crime

I went to di bank today
as I reach di door I hear somebody say
beg yuh a 10 cent mam
I see a man wid a pan in him hand
say di pan was labelled
help the disabled!

went to the church hear parson a preach
give what you have because the lord will give you more
give what you have cuz there is something more in store
give what you have mi seh fi give what yuh have mi seh fi
give what you give what yuh give what yuh have
and him start emulate christ wid di plate
mi tink to myself does di beggar ever
guh inna di holy warmth of the church
no! him just a trod
beggar don't guh church for di fear of di rod
beggar don't guh church for di fear of di rod
beggar don't guh church for di fear of di rod and di shout
get out! get out! get out! get out! get out!

begging is a ting a carry di swing
inna disya time it cyaan be a crime
begging is a ting a ting a carry di swing
inna disya time it cyaan be a crime

it cyaan be a crime

begging is a ting a carry di swing
inna disya time it cyaan be a crime
begging is a ting a ting a carry di swing
inna disya time it cyaan be a crime
begging cannot be a crime
it cyaan be a crime

begging cannot be a crime

CHARLIE BOBUS

What's Black Canadian Poetry?

It's Harriet Tubman
Underground movement to end slavery

It's Dudley Laws marching
so project youths could be free
protesting for equality

It's performing dub poetry
at 365 College Street
where Marcus Garvey
UNIA office used to be

It's traveling to Niagara Falls
channelling the hydro energy
transmuting it into a verse of poetry

It's African poets entering slam
talking about the intricacy
of their past foreparents' slavery
fingers snapping profusely
10s going up
9.9 is the lowest you see

But don't trick yourself
or try to tell me
that black Canadian poetry
is all about slavery

It's more about the self-worth
they stole over sea
by raping the woman constantly

It's shaking the shackles
they placed mentally
poetry mixed with Jazz,
reggae or a hip-hop melody
even dub step

But the message u will see
change your reality
the real McCoy
like the great inventor
poetical patents
new rhyme realms to enter

Setting the stage on fire
with no fear of critique
words so hot
like the fire blamed on Angélique
Afua Cooper writings
the historical facts bequeath

It's a next generation
sprinting words on page
feeling like Donovan Bailey
Gold Medal performance
delivered on stage daily

It's the journey
through Nova Scotia
of George Elliott Clarke doing poetry
rising to be helping the parliamentary

It's a next generation
carrying on the African oral tradition
Poets chanting to bring a solution
100,000 poets strong
resisting against oppression
protesting against imprisonment of the 5 Cuban

It's going to the Harbourfront
as a Jamaican
the joy of seeing our mother of poetry
the Honorable Miss Lou's exhibition

It's the dub poets from the 80s professors and advocates
for the West Indian
after migrating for opportunities
in a faraway land

It's the black history month
poetry educational tour
from Toronto to Vancouver
the youths interested for sure

Poets going in prisons and shelters
speaking to the youths
being their positivity mental helpers
dub poetry spoken word
rap poetry or just poetry pelters

Spoken Word

Based on interviews by Valerie Mason-John
with John Akpata and Tanya Evanson

Is it really possible to say who invented spoken word poetry? For as long as humans have communicated through oral language, they have shaped that language into patterns based on the oral traditions of storytelling and the immediacy of performance.

Tanya Evanson (who has been performing multi-lingually across Canada since 1995, and is the author of six poetry chap books and two spoken wor-l-d CDs) believes spoken word is so vast it is hard to define. "Spoken word is the continuation of the African griot tradition, and poets today bring from the new world, jazz, dub, slam and hip hop. It includes language, rhythm, beat and sounds, and it represents communities."

John Akpata, who performs dub, slam and hip hop under the spoken word umbrella, says it is "the art of speaking, using your voice to educate, entertain and speak to the public. Pre-electricity, we were all performing poetry and telling story. It's what people did."

The Establishment credits people like Hedwig Gorkski, a first-generation Polish American, for originating the term "performance poetry" in the 1980s. However, while she brought recognition to this approach to poetry, performance has ancient roots, and Black people from Africa, the Caribbean and the Diaspora have a huge impact on it.

"Poets like Gil Scott-Heron and Linton Kwesi Johnson and Saul Williams brought about my renaissance of poetic artistic speaking," says Akpata. "They have all worked with musicians to make their poetry accessible."

In Canada, people like Lillian Allen and Clifton Joseph are among the African Canadians who have forged a voice in spoken word. Over the past decade, a generation of younger Black Canadian artists has sprung up. "In 2003 Travis Blackman was a trail-blazer in spoken word," recalls Akpata. "He stoked a fire that warmed a lot of people. In one year he did over three hundred shows. Poets like Wakefield Brewster, Reed IZrEAL Jones, and Scruffmouth really hit me. Dwayne Morgan with When Brothers Speak and When Sisters Speak has also trail-blazed in the 21st century. And now d'bi.young anitafrika has taken spoken word international." Other performers on the Canadian scene today include Shauntay Grant and Anthony Bansfield.

In cities with large concentrations of African Canadians, there has been a particular enthusiasm for spoken word, and Evanson observes the different aesthetics in various communities across the country. "In Montreal, spoken word for African Canadians is exciting because it is experimental, uses different languages and collaborates with other artists. Toronto is more influenced by the urban lifestyle and is more mainstream. Halifax poets often record the Black history of Nova Scotia, and as for Vancouver—well, slam is king. Most spoken word poets are full on with slam."

The stage, the CD, the DVD, YouTube, and self-publication are the "pages" on which spoken-word poets connect to audiences. Such alternative media have allowed the contributions of Black artists to flourish in Canada outside mainstream publishing. The experience of Dwayne Morgan is typical—when he sent his work out to poetry publishers, he met with rejections. Publishers had problems with his use of language, some of his subject matter and how he chose to write about it. So, like many others, Morgan simply responded by publishing his own work.

However, it is on stage where spoken-word artists bring their work alive, using their voices as an instrument to communicate their stories. Such poets are the town crier, the news reporter, social commentator, politician and guardian of society.

But, as Akpata points out, spoken word is part of the continuum with page poetry. "George Elliott Clarke is one of our poets who has prolifically published books, poetry and plays, but you have to see him live. Clarke is a great writer who understands how to use his voice to get people to listen."

In cities where there are large concentrations of African Canadians there has been a renaissance of spoken word since the 21st century. It is vibrant, and new ways of delivering spoken word never fail to entertain.

JOHN ANDREW OMOWOLE AKPATA

Ursula

he wails
again and again and again
day after day after day
the thief on the corner has stolen a lifestyle
that was never meant for him

he stands proudly defiantly openly arrogantly
on his urban garden balcony
surrounded by high rise and condo and glass and concrete
this contradiction
this anomaly
he wails

disrupting the pristine precision and the facade of high end property
in the midst of diplomats and ambassadors and embassies
with audacity he stands unabashedly
he plays flagrantly and growls dastardly
labelled as disruptive and obscene
that messenger that blasts sound to the sky above
he wails

he ascends and descends that pentatonic scale
and inevitably the perfect intonation
that meticulous melody of the internal exacting metronome
fails
he rips the steadyness of sound
he blows solar flares into the clouds and shatters the sky
he wails

like the revelations that john said
he wails
like bagpipes at the grave site at the setting of the sun
he wails
breathing deep and roaring proud
like a giant making his declarations
he wails
shirtless like kuti rallying for revolution
he wails
like a mother wolf who by the full moon searches for lost cubs
he wails
like hendrix riding the feedback from the marshall greenback stacks
the delayed distortion of a cry baby phasing in a fuzz box
he wails
like marley crying tribal to the people
he wails

the vibrato can be felt across the street
down the block
across the pedestrian bridge and echoes into the canal
he bounces sound
up and down the bland facings of his towering neighbours
he splatters them with noise graffiti
he wails

his hands curl like claws and clack the keys
with the secrets of circular breathing
he takes no break he has no pause
the brass bell expands and gets hot
he wails

louder than the church bells at a wedding
he wails
louder than the parliament buildings midnight ringing
he wails
more shrill than the police sirens screaming in the evening
he wails

against the subtle muffled sobbing of
lovers lost at night in the streets of venice
that maze of endless cobblestones and canals
streets unlabelled and shrouded in shadows
the endless labyrinth of streets too narrow to even be alleyways
but there are boats on the grand canal
that are calling their way from the distance
beyond the churches and the museums
that echo that rolls like laughing thunder
he wails

it screams out against the silence of a sleepy city
it is the opposite of a lullabye
it rattles the ears and invades the brain and shakes the heart
a piercing frequency
when you hear it
you can see it
from the blinding bright spot of sparks of brakes dulling the rails of the
    train
the one that arrives only to take your lover away
he wails

and suddenly stops
that moment when all hope is lost
when our loved ones have been put on ships
and finally disappear at the vanishing point upon the horizon
the mast
the stem
the sails
he puts her down
and speaks her name
he wails

TANYA EVANSON

Antigua Antigua

Me las an found me feel profound
Attachment to Antigua, Antigua

Devil's Bridge, Half Moon Bay
Wadadli, min please to greet Antigua, Antigua

Yes me wan dat tide! In dem roots me hide!
Me heritage an me pride, Antigua, Antigua

But me fathahland emotion be so slim / Me wish me could be pull in
Inside a me black skin / Sun inside still strugglin / Antigua / Antigua

Bush tea sugar cane ducanna / New England slave trade patois
Island education inflection / Seulement / Pour moi / Antigua / Antigua

Salt fish chaddock pawpaw / Hausa tribe from Ghana
Conch palm aloe plantain / An a rum ta punch ya head in!

No obeah ye obeah bougainvillea fortune tellah New life North wife
Take I back to black life Antigua / Antigua

Pepperpot an fungee in name only jerk chicken goat watah
Locks in a salt watah sorrel bilimbi lime as a verb Antigua / Antigua

Far from muddahland tight clothes no sweat not like Canada
Cold cold cold cold cold cold fiyah! Antigua / Antigua

Me nah Gretzky / me nah sorry / me nah tank ye / me nah foo'
Antigua Antigua

I an I sun pon de sea / I an I ice pon de tree / I an I me own pickney
I an I me of no me / Antigua Antigua

And Canada / OOOOOH Canada!
She say / Com back ya! Com back ya

The African All of It

I polish myself to be bright and blinding
Some can see me, from others I take sight
When I speak in tongues, none work better than silence
I am listening. I am listening.

The voice can lock but instruments unlock
With the swing of an arm, a pendulum hips
To manipulate breath, control internal chords takes faith
I am listening. I am listening.

Whatever your appearance I am listening
Be it air or cuneiform I am listening
We make love I am listening
Everything turns I am listening
This is our mythology

REED "IZREAL" JONES

The Black Scotians

Every Country, every Province, every City
They always ask me
Where I'm from
So I tells 'em,
I was born on Tuesday in Toronto, Ontario
At Women's College Hospital …
But I'm (Nova) Scotian …
So they ask me where my parents is from
So I tells 'em,
My grand moms is Black & Cherokee from Saskatchewan
My granddaddy's a Maroon from Yard (Jamaica)
And my moms was born in Toronto
But my daddy … my daddy … he's (Nova) Scotian …
So I tell 'em I'm a Scotian …
So they ask me where my daddy's grand ppls is from
And I tells 'em they both Jones, both Scotians,
And I know they lookin' at for me to name
The Caribbean island from which we came & crossed the ocean
So I just tell 'em
Look here, damn near all ppls is (Nova) Scotian
Well … we ain't really Afrikan Canadian, so we aint Afrikan Nova Scotian,
Technically, we are the descends
Of the great grandchildren of kidnapped Afrikans
Who survived the kidnapping, The Middle Passage
The auction blocks, the field, the whips and the chains
But we as Scotian as Mattieu Da Costa speaking Mi'kmaq in 1603
Or the 300 Afrikans living
In the French settlement at Louisburg at the turn of the 18th century
Or the New England planters that number some 150
We are the 3000 plus back loyalists arriving between 1783 and 1786
The 600 Jamaican Maroons who fortified Citadel Hill in 1796
The 2000 Black Refugees who fleed after The War of 1812
The Underground Railroad escapees of the 1820s
And the steel workers from the Caribbean starting in the 1920s.

We are descendant from kidnapped Africans WHO RAN FOR
THEIR FREEDOM
AND FREEMEN WHO FOUGHT FOR THEIR FREEDOM
We carry on their names
And their rich beautiful Afrikan blood flows through our veins
And carries itself with pride in our various skin tones and shades
From Amherst to the Prestons
Yarmouth to Cape Breton
We are the Black Brigade, the Black Pioneers
The No 2 Construction Battalion and William Halls Victoria Cross
We are the African Baptist Church and Richard Preston
Portia White and Viola Desmond
The ancestor's spirit is hand woven
By Edith Clayton into the soul
Of every single Sunday Baptist choir note
We are long one-room, segregated schoolhouses
And the Black Learners Report
We are long bus rides to integrated schools far from home
We are isolated black communities located at dead end stretches of
country road
We are play clothes, school clothes and Sunday's best
We are Madeline Symonds and Dr. Carrie Best
The Clarion's memories stored in our melanin and DNA
We are the Inglewood Players
We are Buddy Daye,
Sam Langford and George Dixon
We are up the road, back the road, down the road
Up home, out home, down home
Downey town Square town Pig town
We got Pa Carvery from William Brown
We are home of the first Race Riots in Shelburne
We are Beechville Days, Canjam, Apex & Black Tournament
Epic wedding parties & family reunions
We better be white by 6 am like Craig Smith
We are stolen lakes for Halifax and Dartmouth to drink
We are well water from iron well water stained sinks

We are Africville warnings signs that read "boil before drinking"
We are the women's auxiliaries
And The Home For Coloured Children
We are Lincolnville where the landfills keep us sick
We are The Black Loyalist Heritage society
And The Black Cultural Centre so the world never forgets we exist
We are The Coloured Hockey League of the Maritimes 1894 to 1936
And after that we are The Halifax Coloured Hockey League until 1940
We are the Wiley sawmill, and Canada's first all
Black volunteer fire department
We are Judge Corrine Sparks and James R. Johnson
We were brought here and left for death
But we survived
So in every Country, every Province, every City
When they ask me
Where I'm from
I tells 'em
My whole family tree
From the roots to the leaves
Are Canadian History
We are The Black Scotians.

MOTION

graf (for heaven11)

You can't catch it
just snatches in frames that
   fly past windows
inscripted in insidious
crevices
scrawled on concrete slabs
of underpass

hush
eyes peeled to feel the pressure
of fingers pressed on spray can tips
aerated shades grow bold in phases
stage impromptu shows at the
sides of the road

It burns
layin on lost walls
for the next eyes
they too will wonder why
these spaces found significance in the
eyes of midnite writer
scribes who
spray legacies of heiros
on the edge of city scapes

      they'll outlast our past
when our last breath escapes
for these dwellers create
carved calligraphies
   scripts on bricks
  tattooed tags stain train's skin
impromptu impressions
impressive dimension
destination, eternal
so lost walls become
heaven

WAKEFIELD BREWSTER

I can

after a decade of delivery on the m.i.c.
unbelievably
people still asking me

what can you DO with poetry?

that question used to make me angry
it used to make me hot
now i tell 'em take a seat
and ask 'em how much time dey got

for you see
with poetry

i can
duly dance down dem same halls of learning where i once had the
  yearning
to be a well accomplished human with a 4.0
but my G.P.A. was sadly way far below
i never got the knack of the educational flow
they made me sit still
so
i
stood
still

i can
comfortably confidently cruise into classrooms where i was coerced to
  create
a cornered captured mental state so i could clearly create a way to
hate my own mind

by my educators
they were edu-haters
they formed a form to form my formative years
tainted with intolerance and a tidal wave of tears
that sailed all of my dreams away from me
for they likened my self-image with one of stupidity
it was all that i heard
and all that i could see

i can
now be free
where i was once imprisoned by a mental prism
my errant splayed thoughts were like hot coloured rocks
endless ammunition for the slings of possibility
but impossibly
all of my targets eluded me
for i was living in the kingdom of "couldn't be me"

i couldn't see the lock
so i didn't need the key
and when they finally let me go
they said you don't know
poetry

i can
versify being victimized into a valiant victory
verify that when you vilify you eventually gotta deal with me
the transformation was tremendous
i took the word stupid and i made it stupendous
i be-gan 'o man hand-le the land 'o language dat languished in
apathetic and anonymous anguish
i did decide to dissect and divide
indefinitely indubitably what diction was doing to me
stab a psyche with a simile and sometimes slip left of centre see
so to step off into a skill-iloquoy
ail the english alphabet with an oral

aural atrocity

i can
wear the face of mental agility
dispel the myth of dental fragility
and proudly embrace my so-called disability
ADD
ADHD
OCD
PTSD

now i've made an acro-nympho-maniac outta me
and never once before have i so ever loved

m.e.

i can
turn my inventive imagination into a physical infatuation
not like sugar
not the hard refined
not like sweetener
not the artificial kind
don't need heroin
cuz i'm a hero in
my own mind
spent some time with my mentality
and what i did find
is

i can
learn

and poetry taught me
when the truth is unfurled
i'm the only one man
who can change my world

so i can do

anything

what can i DO with poetry?

i ask YOU

why don't you tell me?

SCRUFFMOUTH

I am a Claim – Vanrock
*On the occasion of the City of Vancouver Black History Month
Proclamation, delivered in Council Chambers January 31st, 2012*

I am a Claim

Stretching Forth Her Hands across Continental Coastlines
Like a Maverick Reporter Conducting Timely Interviews
to be Printed in Provincial Freedom Papers
across Chronologies and Cultural Spectrums.

Like a Crimson Tide I ride up and over the 49th Parallel
Shedding Flesh like Orange Peels on the Deck of the Commodore.
I will not settle for less than these
Amber Valleys and Green Maple Leafs.

I Ride the Rails like "George"
from the Maritimes of DaCosta
to the Blues of Terminal City
I Smile in the Pale Face of Adversity
and Sleep with my Brothers
Dreaming of a Land Promised to be my Own
after Overseeing Fields of Tobacco, Cotton, Indigo …
Like the Time I took to Smell the Fleur-de-Lis,
Poppies, Roses, Tulips and Violets—
Scents that Travel me to Childhood,
Snuggled on Mother's Continent.

I have these Hands
With Brown Rivers
Scripted in Identified Flesh
Where North & South Rivers Mesh with the Great Seaway
and Empty out into the Bay.

I would not Trade them for the Skins of other Lived Things
and I will use them to Hold my Own
on this Native Land:
Kept and Broken
Written and Spoken
Drummed and Danced.

I am Whirling Furor of Black Cowboy's Lasso,
the Stampede after the Rush,
A Fly in a Pail of Milk,[1]
the Conductor of Symphonies
Wearing Authentic Gold Medals
and Keeping it Real like McCoy.

I am Dropped Gloves off High-Scoring Hands,
Boxing Jabs and Feather Pens,
Ceremonial Swords of Pioneers,
Loaded African Rifles.

I am Clenched Fists of Short-Lived Sprinters,
The Mad Dashes of Hyphenated Titles:
AFRI, AFRO, CARIBBEAN & MORE
a Free African on Canadian Shores

of the Great Black North

Proud

I am.

JASON SELMAN

Sedgwick Ave.

Lend me a psychedelic dream
Lend me pieces of daylight
Lend me a destruction sweeter than anything I can remember
Lend me open sounds, a courtyard, Sedgwick Ave.
Bury this knowledge in sound, a beat that repeats
A rhythm that has a mind of its own
Let the mind grow
Spread to all 5 boroughs like a virus
Black fire, wild stone rhythm for talk
Take over the world
Speak softly, say forever

It was so easy
To know you
Once I began listening to myself
The verse became free
Psychedelic colours and psychedelic graves
Untangling oblivion one limb at a time
Rhythm without and within
Daisies growing wild from the barrel of a gun
Shoot stars

Love is an idle threat
Shouted to the world
Who is not like you?
When delivering themselves to themselves
A glass filled with tears
This venom filled with love
I love her so much
Because she lets me know that I am fading

What is there to own but hearts?
Hearts do all the work
Chain us to betrayal
And on the shadow set us free
Growling midnight, wanting more
Rescue oblivion from me
Given the gift of time
Light years with this glance

Ghetto codes and gray days
The search for search, the sound of sound
Find yourself in flames, evenings on pause
Part of something, apart and in parts
Open the first door
Let yourself in

JEMENI

For Nalo ...

(Originally commissioned for the CBC Canada Reads Program)

Brown Girl in the Ring, Tra la la la la
There's a Brown Girl in the Ring, tra la la la
There's a Brown Girl in the Ring, tra la la la la case
And she looks like a sugar in a plum.
(plum, plum)

Show me your motion ...
Show me your *emotions*,
But if you colour them too loud, they might not fit this crowd.
And as to the exact size of the ring that you're in,
Does it keep you inside Regent Park?
Is it Jane and Finch?
Does it fit inside Jamaica?
"Are you Jamaican?"
"Look I went away on holiday and now I'm blacker n yuuuuu !"
"Do you know Bob Marley?"

Does your story ring true?

And is the ring of your story lined only with
guilt-free Canadian Diamonds?
Or are you one of those lucky brown girls,
whose story is the WHOLE WIDE WORLD.
And whose culture is what she *says* it is!

I am also a Brown Girl in the Ring,
And I *too* sing North America
I *do* still know my heritage,
And nevah mind about my accent. Who are you to tell me that my
stories ain't Canadian?

I am a
Ketchup chip patriot,
A Kraft Dinner baby,
And when American music took over and made radio go crazy,
I remember that it only took *5 Days in May* for Blue Rodeo to save
me.

Somewhere in between Degrassi High and trying to find that damn
Polkaroo,
I went to a predominantly Portuguese school,
And when the home bell rang, we ate African food,
in Chinatown, with greedy mendhi painted hands while my Scottish
friend Haegan promised to make me a friendship band
if I taught him how to stoops, schtueep .... schtuuuuuups!

How much more Canadian can I be?
My mom still calls me *ma petite fille* ...
But the scent of an overripe mango can still take me away,
And what they call a June Plum in Chinatown to me is still a
dyaaam pommecythere!

And don't my Canada taste sweeter that way?

Spent my summers in P.E.I.
I went as a GIRL but left with a crush on a BIE.
I Morenita my way through each Ciao Bella day,
And I sometimes Abooot
But I don't always Eh

And ain't my story still so Canada

Anyway?

TITILOPE SONUGA

Untitled

They said I was
too young
to recognize the tremble
of a talking drum in my throat

said to speak
the language of the elders
I must first
spit the milk teeth from my mouth
make a wish
grow a new set
so I could finally say something
worth chewing on

they asked
how I learned to speak this way
words blooming on my tongue

I'm trying to show you
where I've come from
barefoot dreams and dusty roads
running with a pocket full of stories
that began first in my mother's mouth
scratched raw from
the inside of her womb

I imagine I entered the world
with poetry on my fingertips
strumming the chords
of a melody that began
long before me

a legacy of words
that plant themselves
in the base of my throat

and dare me to choke
or breathe
and this is breathing

every time I throw my voice
across a room
that asks me to be anything
but black and woman

every time I show you my heart
so that we can begin to name
the vital artery that binds us
by blood

I reclaim my tongue
to speak of the storms
we have weathered
the oceans we carry in our veins
to remind us of the tides
that brought us here

washed ashore
with nothing but this history
dripping from our skin
a legacy written in song
all the stories caught from
our mother tongue
to re-tell again

and this is what
divine revolutions are made of
how you become me
and I
you

daughters
of a long line of women
gripping bullets between their teeth
stifling cries while catching
babies by candlelight

every tremble in my voice
carries the rhythm of your pulse
every story I have ever told
your heart already knows

OSAZE DOLABAILLE

I Did Not Choose My Name

I did not choose my name:
I didn't plan the fatigue
that can only result from an obsessive need
to make some more money
or never be late
Could I have foreseen that on this special date
a suggestion would lead me to seek a new name?
Well, I seemed to have known I would not be the same
once the plague of self-doubt had been cleansed from my soul
and my fragmented pieces
restored to their whole
that the elder within me would finally hold sway
as a formless anxiety drained slowly away
and when every last bit of self-hatred was gone
the self-love that replaced it would never go wrong

My big sister had been there
she already knew
The name change was something that I had to do
so I began searching to see what I could find
something safe, and familiar
was what I had in mind
But "Osaze" was different
it vibrated to me
I wrote down some others but knew then it would be
the one name I would carry the rest of my days
Recollecting that moment, I'm still quite amazed
I couldn't feel myself with it
it felt awkward to say
but I knew from the meaning it had to be the Way
For my Creatress assured me with one simple name
it is okay to try
I am loved just the same

As I stand at the edge now preparing to fly
up to heights never reached
out for things never tried
I'm reminded of how all of this came to be
I did not choose my name, no
my name—it chose me

Black Boy

Ah see ya over yonder on Blue Berry Hill.
Smilin with those pearly whites,
showing those muscles off,
ya pants real tight.
ah see ya black boy,
stay cool tonight!

Oh now ya moving up in so-ci-e-ty,
ya have eyes for a gal like me?
Go cross the sea, stop ya foolin.
I'll stay here while ya get ya schoolin.

Ah rememba ya black boooy,
ya long slender neck with strong jawline.
Ya hips moving to the drum beat.
Ah rememba what ya look like,
walking down Taylor Street.

Ah know ya black boy
no one knows ya better than me.
We shared a lot in them blue berry fields.
raw pleasure, love that was real.

Ah hear ya gra-du-ated,
become ed-u-ca-ted.
Promised, you would come for me,
so I'm waiting patiently.

Yo momma says, ya comin home,
so I got me a pretty dress on loan.
Ah'l meet ya at the station,
ya can tell me all bout ya education.

I'm gonna grab ya by the hand,
let everyone know yaah still my man.
Ah here the whistle blowin,
pretty soon, you'll be a showin.

Now there ya are in a fine suit,
with a pretty girl, lookin really cute.
What about me? did ya forget about me?
What did ya say? *excuse me MISS???*
How can ya treat me like this!

KOMI OLAFIMIHAN A.K.A. POETIC SPEED

My Muse

My muse,
Are you aware we composed a poem twice a day in our sleep
Until we fell in love face first?
Now, the residue of our love will serve as inspiration to composers,
Those who write symphonies and songs
In unison with the sun
Until the moon decides to eclipse out of jealousy.
I would not apologize for the casualties of our happiness.
Countless numbers of hearts needed to be shattered as a sacrifice to
  Venus,
Now the multitude of disgruntled lovers
Watch from a distance, across the pond in Quebec
Waiting for our energy to evaporate like snow and come down as
acid rain
They are unaware we have secretly transcribed our story into
Arabic, Portuguese and French
Sumerian symbols and hieroglyphics
Romantic love languages they will never be able to comprehend

Baby
At midnight,
Meet me beneath the golden arches
Let us bask in burger grease and talk about fries and onion rings
from A & W,
While we plot to steal and destroy
Those noisy contraptions that produce those terrible
McDonalds lattes
An insult to the taste buds of a finesse coffee drinker like myself
You,
The illegitimate daughter of Neptune,
Sing me into existence.
If I could,
I would write you back to life,
Paint your soul between your skin and flesh
Carve your bones from limestone and bury your dreams in the soil
of your potential
And watch it grow into a garden of success

My muse who is patient enough to cut open my palms and read my veins
Likes her eggs with the shell still intact
Always carries a razor-sharp haiku in her back pocket like an
antique switch blade
My cousins from Saturn call her "slash"
Slash, she conceals a loaded pistol in her mouth and plays Russian
roulette with her tongue
God damn.

Baby
They say smoking is a drug
I say "not smoking" is a drug
I "not smoked" until I began to hallucinate.
Then it came to my attention,
There is something grotesquely beautiful in the art of washing dishes,
The careless soaking of the sponge,
The intricate structure of the foam as it rises to the top of the sink
Like some sort of fantasy dragon egg waiting to hatch fluffy
butterflies
That makes me feel warm and fuzzy on the inside
Interesting, I may adopt her method of dishwashing
Elegance in the mundane
Mundane in her elegance

My muse
Have you noticed
How the scar on my left arm has marked me as a vagabond
Roaming the streets aimlessly like the unwanted bastard child of an
earthquake and hurricane
Smelling like casino chips and child labor
Begging an ex-lover to birth me cute puppies since she called me a dog
I would rather plunge myself naked in the rapid rivers of your past
Unearth the secrets buried somewhere between the seven seas,
The Great Wall of China and the light that exudes from the pores of
your skin.
My muse

DEANNA SMITH

I Ain't Gonna Study War No More

barbie
u …. biquitous
symbol of the north american standard of beauty
you're fired
i never hired you in the first place
i acquired you in an arms race
i didn't know i was in
i only had to be born for the war to begin
it goes like this
if you look like barbie
you're beautiful
so you win
i was losing a race i didn't know i had entered
mentored by women who had lost their race and their war
long before me
so naturally
and quite casually
my hair became a casualty
of
"mummy, perm it …
it's ugly"
i thought i needed better artillery
and the women in my family supported me
black and blue and purple hearted as they all were
from their own time in the infantry
they sat me down and did the deed repeatedly
i became a soldier in the army of dark and lovely
for a while i held my own against the enemy
that being
new growth
how ironic
i swerved the natural weapons of mass destruction
like humidity and rain
endured the pain of the occasional chemical burn
because if you want to be a woman
you have to earn that right, right?

i thought i was deflecting the bombs
barbie and her soldiers would hurl
i eventually discovered the jheri curl
and marched greasily through my teens
unaware
that the battle i was fighting
was not with my hair
i was about twenty
when it occurred to me
that it had been about a decade
since i had touched a barbie
that she really didn't have anything to do with me
and that i could step out of this myth
i could become a very active pacifist
i started to resist
i cut off my hair
and bought an afro pick with a fist
i stopped fighting
i started inciting others
to lay their arms down
to heal their harmed crown
and stop believing in what was never a child's game
i wasn't even in kindergarten
and i already knew her name
barbie
it's time she lost her job
trying to rob little girls
of the right
to begin their lives
without losing a fight
so tonight
i'm doing what's right
and required
barbie
u …. biquitous symbol of the north american standard of beauty

YOU'RE FIRED

RYAN BURKE

Historically Present Ghosts

From this lesson
   I take the most
Listening intently
I hear the elders
Speak tales
   Of historically present ghosts
Telling my peers
That after years of struggle
Our generation
Is the only one
That remains caged freely
With no one
To step forward
And carry on our legacy
   The torch bearer
   Of our ancestry

No longer do we remain as cubs
As it becomes our time
To become the Lions
Within our community
And like those before us
Teach those after us
The tales of our experiences
Remaining true to the African Proverb
   Illustrating ourselves
   As true Historians

You see
They tell me of
Mathieu Dacosta
And how Africville became to be
   In Nova Scotia
Following the "North Star"
To the "Great White North"

Seeking Freedom
With instrumental figures
Like Harriet Tubman
    And Richard Pierpoint
The Quakers
Alongside various
    Movers and Shakers

Remembering
Brown v. The Board of Education
Yet ignorant to the fact that
Segregated schools
Were also a part of
    This Nation
Until folks like Lincoln Alexander
Wilma Morrison
And the Honourable
Jean Augustine
    Struck back
And fought for the liberties
To which many take liberty
Which is why Afua Cooper
Reminded us
Of how it used to be
By once again
Opening our eyes
To a sad reality
With her written work
Entitled
    "The Hanging of Angélique"

As Dudley Laws
Fought for us all
    Regarding police brutality
Remembering it was
Just the other day
That my "kin folk" said
"Enough is enough"
And valiantly took
    To the streets

Yet still shadowed
By our neighbours to the South
As our great nation
Belittled our situation
And broadcasted
    The "Rodney King" beatings
Stating, we're nothing like them
As they remain the "Melting Pot"
While we remain
Beautifully multi-cultural ·
    Like a stain glassed pane "imagery"
But like my father always says
Don't throw stones
In a glass house
Unless a great mess
    Is what you aim to see

Now they're telling me
That my peers and I
Suffer from "Apathy"
But how can one truly resist
If all we hear from our supporters
That rocking the boat
Is not something
    They permit
You see
I live in a country
That tells me
Compared to way back when
I have equality
But what is equality
Without identity?!
And what is identity
When often it is seen
Simply in zoned communities
Putting the pieces
Of this scattered puzzle together

So that I may ask
    My question appropriately
If placed in a zoned community
Am I a product of
    Disenfranchised unity?!
Or a prime example
Of an
    Illusionary unified society?!

Because not much
Is in a name
Rather, the clothes I wear
And my ethnicity
    Are what speak for me
Leaving the syllables
That reverberate off my tongue
Soundful
    Yet mute to many
Which is why the leaders
Of my generation
    Continue to go unseen
As easily
We cast our sights
Solely on those
    Masked Men in Our Society
Presently Historical Ghosts
As the Revolution
Has no longer become …
… Newsworthy

ASHLEY ALEXIS MCFARLANE

The Re-Image Urge

I wonder
If at least
The moon will have my back
When I tell her
That more than anything I want
To see myself recreated
As a child with this
Bad
Nappy
Kinky hair
Thick lips
And skin as dark
As the sky
She hangs in

I want to recreate that woman
That reminds you
Of slavery
The Middle Passage
Home
Your mom
Red fingers
As you sat between her legs
She styled your dome piece
I want to recreate
Little black babies
Who will be loved
Equal and whole
With full lips
Celestial eyes
And unabridged noses

Know I
Want to recreate Africa
When Egyptians were Nubians
And not just Arabian invaders
Breeding the blackness out
Of Sudanese bodies
A mentality too ripe with
Hate her
And assimilate
"The universe wants us to
Be all mixed up and happy
Just like the yin and yang"
A blue-black gorgeous man
Told me
Once
I want to create diversity
Where we can all be us
Equal and whole
And not be blinded by a system
That still needs a serious injection
Of some soul (r power too)

I want to recreate the rage that says
Stop chaining black bodies
For material gain
And blaming gang violence
Yet ignoring the pain
On the faces of the poor
A pain that resonates through all races
Across shores
Across shores
I want to recreate

The re-image urge

Re-emerge

ADELENE DA SOUL POET

Da Brotherman

This is a true story:
This young man got sentenced to 80% of 20 years.
For robbing the pizza man.
Yeah like many young black men
He'd been targeted on the streets before.

He played basketball for the police department youth team and one day
the young man that gave him a ride to the game had a gun in his car.
Juvenile detention for one month—for being in the car …

My boy is Black, and that meant Prison.
Arrested a second time—he gets
Level 4
Prison in California, the highest level.
He was so afraid, and his mother heartbroken and so afraid for her son.

In California the brotherman went down for 18 yrs … not life / … that
wasn't enough so they gave him 2 strikes! / They slammed him on a
first offense, / at 18 they gave him 18 robbing him of a fair defence /
So there he went with his scared young self behind them prison
walls / promising his mama to write once a week, stay strong and
stand tall.

He kept his word … he was never a gang member never into drugs /
but the shit behind them walls was deep deep deep dirty down … that
what it was! / A Christian a Muslim or affiliate with gangs the
choice was his to make. / He met and was guided through by the big
man Mustafa of the Muslim faith,
Islam.

Mustafa was very well known and respected thru-out the
penitentiaries. / His was the faith you did not cross, Mustafa was the
man you see! / He'd been in that hell for 20 yrs he knew the harsh
reality. / He took brotherman under his wing … taught him how to
walk the walk and talk the talk … taught him how to pray / to Allah!
How to exercise to stay / strong, how to build up the mind to keep
thoughts positive taught him how to survive. Survive in that fucked
up hell. He taught him right … and he taught him well! / Now

brotherman soaked the knowledge in like a sponge to water … / the system couldn't brainwash him—oh no! / He has the inner and the outer strength the self-respect and the confidence / doing his time with his mama in mind!

With 10 yrs down, brotherman and Mustafa got separated by the system. / But they hooked up again in another state pen … to watch each other's back / and again they transferred brotherman … Mustafa died in prison shortly after that!!

A sad day it was for brotherman … and his mama … when she heard the news, was truly shook up! / Mustafa for her had taught her son how to survive. / Survive in a place that's really messed up … So she cried!! / Now brotherman stayed strong remembering what he was taught. He's smart!! / He walks on by with his head held high Mustafa Muhammad is in his heart … / that's right! He carried on mindin his business in that California State Pen.

He wrote to his mama sayin … "I was thinking Ma—now I'm the veteran! / So I know what to do and you're not to worry I'm a strong man mama you see / I'm big as a house it's not fat it's muscle mama nobody fucks with me / I outsmart the guards with intelligence the inmates old young they dumb / I ain't here to socialize. I'm a do my time with my mama in mind. / I'm a do my time with my mama in mind. I'm a do my time and run!! / But while I'm here I decided to sit on back with my own lessons, / mama I'm taking knowledge in from each and every direction./ I can't help myself I can't stop either it's like feedin a hungry brain / and mama you know when I walk up outta here, ain't nothing gonna be the same!"

Now brotherman was makin sense and soundin pretty cool / he say … "mama let me give you an example. I'm a take you to penitentiary school!! / This is where one keeps to oneself, minds they own, only they own business. / What you see and what you hear is kept very privately … this ain't city jail / This ain't city jail … it's the fuckin penitentiary!! Now these motherfuckers up in here, the rules the laws of the California State Pen … /Segregate, humiliate, / try and intimidate the inmate! / Watch your back cause you ain't got no friends!"

"But mama you keep me sane, this much is very true / you taught me how to be who I am and I am so thankful to you. / I found some positive in the negative just like you said!! / And I got the power of knowledge all in my head! /For breakfast mama this is what I do. / I read a book from cover to cover you see / it gives me power it gives me strength it gives me energy, / and if the appetite ain't satisfied, I'll have a lil dessert. / Mama I'm doing 5-600 pull-up push ups and sit ups, all on this penitentiary dirt!! / You tell me time ticks forward and it never ever goes back, / I hold onto those words mama cause you are so right about that!! / So 3-4 more yrs of time, and it cannot exceed / you know when I walk up outta here I will succeed, / I will succeed!

I love you mama!

da brotherman"

TEEANNA MUNRO

The Harlem Nocturne

Oh Man!
I can still remember the very Night
when I first heard the Harlem Nocturnes
I can still hear the music

It was a Friday March 1963
I can remember the month
because I just moved in from Oklahoma
and the forecast was
COLD
colder than a lonely woman in heat

and man was I hungry so
I headed to a slick chicken joint
on the corner of union and main and

from three blocks away
I swear
three blocks away
my frozen ears were thawed by Vancouver's own
Thelma Gibson

sweet to the ear singing
I got it bad and that ain't no good
and you know she don't lie
because in that moment
I had it bad but it sure felt good

forgetting my hunger pains
I went to where I could get some real satisfaction
343 East Hastings Street
The Harlem Nocturne

and that scene was Thick!
for three dollars
you were guaranteed a good time

no liquor
but everyone was still
lookin' good 'n actin' bad
just sassy and struttin'
that joint was jumpin'

soft lights
smoked filled air
heavy with fried chicken
you don't even need to eat
for that smell was so thick
it made you full

footprints painted all over the ceilings
I remember thinking
this place must be hot
because these dancers
ain't got no boundaries

The Band
Ernie King
Mike Taylor
Chuck Logan
that place was alive
floor dancers dressed to the nine

after all my years at Harlem
all I can say to you is
there was laughter
man there was always laughter
just thick and light

So in the words of the Great Ernie King

"Ladies and Gentleman, that's all y'all"

SIOBHAN BARKER

The Call

My pulse quickened at the sound of the ring tones.
Would he be home? Please be home.

"Hello" he says.

I hadn't quite figured out what to say.

I could mention the way that my chest tightened, hovering between breaths, with
just the sound of his voice.

I could mention the slight sheen forming on my lower lip as memories of a kiss
played with my senses.

I could tell him of hungry sessions when I drew pleasure, remembering the paths
of fingers travelling over hot moist valleys, secreted between thighs.

I could say how his voice held a promise of strength and a whisper of urgency
not to be denied.

I could breathe in and revel in the distant echo of his sensual scent, remembering
being roused to a point that threatened both our resolves.

I lick my lips
I tremble
Ah, the memory of passion's salty-sweet taste

"Hello. Is anyone there?" he asks,

I took a deep breath, pushing back the whirlwind of wayward images.

"Hi, it's so good to hear your voice."

My 2 Cents

If you want my 2 cents … Vote
And don't let them watch sex on TV
Don't let them watch sex on TV
Don't want these kids being perverts
You can turn on the TV, let them watch the murders
Or just buy them video games, Let them practise to murder
Or just send them out on these city streets and watch them get murdered

But I don't see nothing wrong with sex on TV
As long as you don't fall off
But I believe that I like sex
More than I like murdering people
Don't judge me … it's a life choice

And another thing …
Trailer trash Bitch America
Done shaved her bush and got herself a black man
But I still see the probability of problems
Prolonging the planning process of one's personal prosperity
No grants, No government bailouts
I … work for a living

Re – Cess – Shun (a period of reduced economic activity.)
The name of my pocketbook's unauthorized biography
Not sure if I want Denzel or Will Smith to play me in the movie
But tell the tax man
Get your hands out my pocket man

Number one on the bestsellers list
If Oprah mentions it
But that's one for the books that will never get read
Just thrown at you

Just download it on your bbm or I-phone
Cus it's the shit yo
And for those that missed it
Check out You-tube, and stream for the video
30,000 hits in the last 5 minutes
And I'm telling you Vote, It's the shit

The world we live in … in REAL time
A processed reality, broadcast back to you on TV
Where you too, can be Paris Hilton's BFF
Back pack shit like Kanye, be Conscious like KRS,
Poetic like Mos Def … RIGHT what's left
Hoping that Obama isn't killed
So that he doesn't end up
As one of the next dead presidents
On the American dollar bill

But who is paying attention,
And what is it costing you. Vote
Cus housing that's affordable
Don't have the same ring
As Profitable's … K- ching

So now the re-vital-ization … Has MORE
Coffee shops and condos on corners
Than liquor stores in ghettoes
And I guess that's a good thing
For the economy
Probably just a con on you and me
As they con those into getting condos
Better cost of living, but what does it cost to live in
The Sky Box
Where … you don't … feel like a player
Or even … part of the game

Trying to keep up with the Joneses
That don't even acknowledge you … or know your name
You should be working to live, and not living to work
And that's probably just me, being cliché … Vote

And if you asked for my two 2 cents
It will cost you 5 cents like grocery bags
Cus my 2 cents is valuable
And in these hard economic times
I just can't afford to give it away
But don't Harper on it

The lesser of two evils
Sex on TV or the lowest voter turnout in history
This is Canada, the place we call home
But my real question is
When we gonna get a Black Prime Minister of our own?

NEHAL EL-HADI

Sudan's Civil Divorce

What happens when what you believe existed
Gets taken away from you
Torn apart and twisted?

What happens when the ground you used to stand on
Quivers crumbles and turns into
Something you can't even land on?

A promised beginning now got broke apart false start
We forgot the price of death bleeding and broken hearts
Forgot about fathers who lost sons forgot about our chosen one
Forgot about history and celebration
Forgot legacy and the wealth of our nation

Situation unstable.

Mismatched elements from a historic periodic table.

There should be no surprise at the demise of something that never was
But even at the end of a forced marriage there's hope for just cause
And a child of divorce is never the same keeps on feeling the pain
The outlines of a thing once known vanished no longer remain

A love maintained.

Kept breathing for an imaginary illusion
The known world shattered in the wake of this inevitable conclusion
Violence in resolution.
We believed in permanence hope blinding us
To the consequences of a group delusion.
Faith in security misguided execution.

Tell me what happens when the lines that defined you
Are drawn on desert sand
Erased by a gust the wind blew.

AKHAJI ZAKIYA

we are

we are ...
fluid   forming space into stories
hybrid   healing thru influences
immigrant & indigenous
universal syncopating blends
dialects, accents, imagination
voiced mosaics
Brand, Allen, Elliott
foundation for
Young, Morgan, Kamau
and beyond

we are ...
diasporic deep
renaissance rhythmic
streaming slams, snaps and smiles
on
stages, pages
anywhere we hear
roots rocking our ready

ready?

IAN KAMAU

Black Bodies

In the shadow of the gun the unsung live away from the sun / the river of peace it's often the shallowest one / though once some hung to silence our voices / violence and riots for denying our choices / now the choice it's for black boys to fall like rain / bullets make a body fold like paper cranes / our lives at a time both sacred and profane / and black folk selling black folk crack cocaine / and the business is good / customers come to visit if you live in the hood / so now we love the ghetto we believe it's our home / the streets are our kingdom the corner our throne / we're like flies in the fibres of spiders webs / trapped / taking orders like Simon says / we no longer court the truth but seek a bullet instead / 'cause the world barely cares if we're alive or dead

Like stakes in the heart bullets like bats tend to fly after dark / so we make sure the children are home from the park / a shame, everyday another name to discuss / flood the streets with their guns and they blame it on us / always at the back of the bus as they say / Jane made the front page after boxing day / these guns you can get them off the streets off the shelves / so the youth make the purchase to protect themselves / parents unaware of what the new reality is / tragically a catastrophe where families live / and many black boys becoming men on their own / you won the lottery if you got a father at home / so we find the wrong influence looking for a father figure / don't see the irony in why we call each other "nigger" / it kills the concept of a brother or a sister / no surprise we occupy both sides of the trigger / standing in wonder / under the cover of the sun / listen the distant thunder of the summer of the gun / put the truth right in front of our eyes we don't see it / that's why these young brothers say "peace" but don't mean it / fighting wars unaware of what we're dying for / foolish, the streets they ain't mine or yours / so we cry and say goodbye to the lives we know / 'cause as fast as they come they go

Like playing with flame / kids are killers now they're making a name / only some but our community it's taking the blame / though the killer knows the blame is essentially his / most folks are unaware of who the enemy is / it's distorted whenever a life is aborted before its time / and our kind sure can't afford it / still it seems that the dream of the streets won't cease / but we know that blessed are those that make peace / guns make a mockery of the life we treasure / leaving flesh twisted like treble clefs in a measure / calling out loud screaming "love" we can't say it enough now / we're smearing our blood on the pavement / giving the same pain / making the same claims / living the same shame / killing to maintain / because we don't trust we doubt first / a life without worth it's prone to outbursts / so we're still dying / only the killer has changed / Africans once in the waves the worth of a slave / now the dope on the street is the rope on the tree / and these guns are the box kicked from under our feet / the hate is not replaced it's the fists in the fight / respect for life it's rotting before it's ripe / we didn't choose these ghettos, favelas and slums / but it seems they made these Goddamn guns … for black bodies

crystal gale

i was the nappy-kinky-headed-blackey
skid-marked-tar-brown-bag ecru-coloured-baby
with tough thick short naps
and tight coils that stood straight up
(a strong gust of wind couldn't knock 'em down)

i bought thumbed-through yellow-paged
harlequin romances for 25 cents at church bazaars
then wondered why my "tresses" weren't
auburn wavy long silky and cascading
like all the fine porcelain-skinned heroines

i anchored bath towels to my head.
secured t-shirt collars around my forehead.
swung cotton side to side; practiced for hours
envisioned crystal gale strands grazing
my shoulders lower back calves heels.

with an unhardened heart
i sat frozen still by the almond electric stove
eyes opened wide in anticipation of the
greased red hot comb of sizzling salvation

lord!

we crimp curl roll slick-back braid
twist double-strand twist blow-out 'fros
we lock bond glue cornrow
we chini-bump bantu-knot sister-lock low 'fro
synthetic human yaki weave texturize

we waved loose coarse and fine
we jheri curl leisure curl stiff curl whirl
old stockings cap wave caps press and silk wraps
we steam colour highlight
deep-condition wash leave-in condition

we pick plait brush mousse moisturize oil infuse, diffuse
we comb style gel our baby hairs—artfully
cover 2nd-degree curling iron flat iron burns—skillfully
we break thin bald thick fall out in clumps
we sheen spray set sit under dryers for hours

we 1B/27 and platinum on any given Sunday
we sun-in cover-up rinse bleach and dye
we l-y-e and l-i-e lie "our hair is our beauty"

we been everythang
housed everythang
wept everythang.

we fingers thick tough calloused beyond cream
we rock limp carry spring walk and thang
we crash get up leap crawl stand
we scraping by without formal education
we scraping by ph.ded with plenty work experience

we been the nappy-kinky-headed-blackeys
skid-marked-tar-brown-bag-ecru-coloured-babies
we manageable we complex we perplexed
we pick apart our physical and mental daily
still praying convinced what we got ain't enough

"lord yemoja universe jah allah give me (fill in the blank)
and i'll be alright"

damn it
we were born all right.

it was only yesterday that lungs wrangled cries, eyes wrestled
tears, flesh grappled whips, and mystics cultivated hope from
despair. these are the brighter days—the ones delivered by all
who jumped were drowned, sharks feasting, who dangled
mangled, blood hounds feasting. ashes scattered flesh ablaze,
these are the brighter days. rejoice.

JEAN PIERRE MAKOSSO

Love You Yet Again

Love from the mother
Given to the child
Child grows up becomes a man
Sows his seed and grows so wild
Born of woman born in pain
He has forgotten whence he came
Woman knows and woman cries
I will love you yet again

Love from the mother
Given to the child
Endure the pain that rends the skies
I will bear you up once more
Though dark of Earth you would explore
And when it is to hell you go
I'll be there to take the blow
I will love you yet again

Love from the child
Given to the mother
Shining rainbow flying spirit
Spreads the light spreads the truth
Came from Earth born on Earth
Connection mother through your eyes
I see friendship
I will love you yet again

Your love mother
Given to me
Is a reflection in my mirror
Is a shadow hiding in me
Mother cares mother loves
I'll spread the word around the world
No matter what no matter how
I will love you yet again

Slam

Based on interviews by Valerie Mason-John with Oni the Haitian Sensation,
Dwayne Morgan and 2010 World Slam Champion Ian Keteku

Slam is less a form of poetry than "an event with a form of poetry in it,"
says Dwayne Morgan. It is a competition, where work isn't validated by a
publisher but by an audience's judgement. Unlike other forms of spoken-
word performance, the use of music, costumes and props is forbidden—
contestants have their voices and only their voices to sway opinions.

"The oral tradition of competing with words is very old. It was how
governments were once run, and still are," says Keteku.

However, a successful slam poem is still poetry—it depends on cadence,
rhythm and personality. It can be anything from a rant to a social
commentary to a sophisticated poem that would also work on the page.

The invention of the slam competition is credited to a Chicago
construction worker, Marc Smith, in 1984. Since then slam has spread
like a bush fire on the continents of North America, Asia, Europe and
Australia, with world championships. And it has a special appeal for
young Black poets. Morgan believes that in Canada this is because Black
Canadians are still at the periphery of Canadian society, and that much
slam poetry concerns itself with identity and gender politics. He says "…
slam lends itself to immediate validation and gratification. And this is a
place where the Black experience can be validated."

Canadian poets like Andrea Thompson were early participants in U.S.
competitions, but the first slam in Canada is believed to have been held in
Vancouver in 1996. Dwayne Morgan held the first-ever slam in Toronto
in September 1999. "I had no idea what slam poetry was," he says. "I
received an email from Philadelphia inviting me to a slam, so I thought I
may as well go. I took my mom's van and drove down to Philly. As soon
as I saw it I knew the community back home would love it. Many of us
had grown up on hip hop and dance hall battles. The idea of poetry as a
competition was exciting for me."

The slam competition format is clearly defined. Poets have a maximum
of three minutes (with a ten second grace) to deliver their work. The host
selects five judges from the audience who have no relationship to the
contestants. They are briefed to be consistent, using criteria of content,
performance and delivery to decide on a score between zero and ten
immediately after each poet performs. A "sacrificial poet" performs before

the contest begins; judges score this performance to establish a guide for the poets to follow. A competitor is penalized for exceeding the time limit by having half a point docked from their total score for every ten seconds they go beyond the ten second grace. Highest and lowest scores are dropped before calculating the poet's total.

There is now a well-established community of Black Canadian slam poets, including people like Eddy Garnier, Gemini, Heron John, Unblind, Leviathan and Eddy da Original One (who has also been a historian of the slam poetry scene). Ottawa and Vancouver were pioneers of the Canadian slam movement, sending teams to the National Poetry Slam in Chicago, in August 2003. Many of these participants were African Canadians, including John Akpata, Garmamie Sideau, Oni the Haitian Sensation, and Anthony Bansfield aka Nth Digri. In 2010 Black Albertan Ian Keteku became the Slam World Champion.

Oni The Haitian Sensation was the first poet to compete in both French and English at Canadian slam festivals. She was also Ottawa's first slam poetry champion in January 2001. In 2005, York University called her "Canada's first slam poetry academic."

She points out the sometimes paradoxical nature of the slam community, which often deals head-on with racism. "Black slams often denounce racism perpetuated by white people. When I was at the National Poetry Slam held in Chicago in 2003, Puerto Rican poet Shaggy Flores from the Nuyorican and I experienced colourism; he was considered "too light" to participate in Black slams, although he identified as Black, and I was too "dark" to participate in the Latino Slam, although I'm also Cuban."

Regardless of such politics (and in spite of the turned-up noses of certain old guards), slam is a flourishing forum for expression by Black Canadian poets. Slam has no establishment guarding it with locked doors. It is a radical revolution where poetry belongs to the general public, local communities and young people. Anybody can take part in a slam.

IAN KETEKU

Laptop Love

I want to open you up and turn you on
Push all the right buttons just to get you going
Your kisses are like ellipses I am caressing your backspace
We escape to a space bar none
This function got my knee caps locked

I don't care if you are square
Nobody's in here, just me and you and clips from Youtube
I wanna control your heart beat
Never ctrl, alt, delete
But sometimes I have to when you freeze

You are getting old, Miss Vista
I miss the old Miss Vista

You used to go where I go and be where I be
Join me to Starbucks even though you don't drink
You used to stay up all night when I had a paper due
You would fly with me on planes
And you would walk me to school

You never used to care when the young children wanted to play
Or when my friends would come over and say,
"Eh yo Ian, your computer really sucks, dude."

But you are a getting old, Miss Vista …

Mac?

Mac is just a girl I do video editing on
Listen baby, it's a recession right now and I cannot afford a Mac
Let me tell you the truth: I do video editing on her, but I write poetry
on you.

I am sorry I cheated on you
I borrowed my friend's computer
It is small, black and has this cute little apple right on—
No, no baby I am not calling you fat
I am just saying you have a bit more RAM than the others

I am sorry I banged you around
I am sorry I dropped you on the ground
I am sorry I spilt hot chocolate on you even though you don't drink
After, I tried to enter my home but the keys were stuck

I am sorry I swore at you.
I called you a stupid piece of shift.

But you haven't been that great to me either, Miss Vista
You fall asleep whenever you want to
You shutdown whenever you want to
You pause so much you should get an apostrophe

One time I tried to connect with you
And you're all like,
"uh huh, Honey, I'm offline right now."
I said, "okay."

And I know you don't want me to say it
But you got those viruses

I don't care from who or whatever
All I am happy is that my friend Norton was able to help us out

Remember the good old days, Miss Vista
Remember the days where I wanted to tab your asterisk
Or put my USB stick into your hard drive
Oh those were the good old days

But you are getting old, Miss Vista

So sleep, Miss Vista
Sweet dreams, Miss Vista

But tomorrow please, please come back as the old Miss Vista

Laptop Love

DWAYNE MORGAN

The Academy Awards

I was being me;
Not on set, not acting,
Just doing what I do.
Maybe my headphones were too big.
Maybe the way my head bobbed to my music
Was offensive.
Maybe my pants were too baggy.
Maybe my skin was just too dark;
Or maybe they make the sidewalks smaller
On this side of Vancouver.
Either way
It apparently wasn't big enough
For the both of us.
As I approached,
She stepped aside,
Clenched her purse,
And stood frozen in place.
As soon as I walked past,
She was back on her path,
And I felt as though
I was in a movie or a dream.
Part of me wanted to turn around
And start walking behind her,
But that would only give relevance
To her insignificance;
Part of me wanted to stop too,
Right in front of her;
This would be the crux of the plot,
Where the tension builds;
The pivotal climax,
As we waited to see who would make the next move.
Part of me wanted to call her on her actions,
But I feared that she might soil herself
If I came at her with pens blazing.
It's amazing that this attitude is still alive.
Instead of exercising any of those options,
I simply walked by,
Playing my role,

Because as Black people,
We constantly act as though we don't care,
As though we aren't hurt,
As though we aren't angry.
We are always acting to save face.
I can never be more than the sum of my experiences,
And while she can never make me or break me,
There's still a permanent scar on my spirit,
Because I can have university degrees,
But I'm still just seen as a nigger;
I can run my own business,
But I'm still just seen as a nigger;
My passport looks like a sticker book,
And I'm still just seen as a nigger.
So I keep acting,
Because it's the only way to maintain my sanity,
In a society
That judges my worth against White people's fantasies,
Their options of who they want, and expect me to be.
But sorry,
I won't be your sexual terrorist,
Mandingo black cock that terrifies and intrigues you;
I will not be your less than,
Your other, your different;
You are not the standard by which my worth is measured.
I won't give you the pleasure of being
The gang banging hood,
Intimidating you as you walk by;
Not today,
I only hang on writers' blocks.
Today I will be the defiant jack in the box
That won't let you box him in.
I will put on an act
Worthy of acclaim and smashing box office records.
Yes, I have issues, and a colour complex,
Because not a day goes by,
When I'm not reminded of the skin that I'm in,

And you don't know the psychological,
And spiritual trauma,
Of constantly having to justify your existence,
Your location, and your presence.
Yes, I am a Canadian,
Yes, my parents were immigrants,
But who gives you the power
To think that it's ok to ask?
So we act,
Better than those in Los Angeles diners,
Waiting on their big break.
But your looks of fear,
And surveillance cameras
Are the only paparazzi that we know,
Because if we don't create value for you,
Or validate you in some way,
We really don't matter,
And we've got this acting thing
Down to a science.
We acted like we cared
Before we burnt down the cane fields.
We acted like we loved you
Before we poisoned your food.
We acted like you mattered
When we took care of your homes
And your children;
Now we teach acting lessons
To nanny's from the Philippines
Who clean up after you as a means to an end.
We act as though we believe you
When you speak of us being equals,
Maybe true reparations
Was Michael Jackson owning the Beatles.
We act as though we're exotic,
When someone who looks like you
Finds us worthy of love.
We act as though we can carry the world,
When we're really just fed up,

And when the Academy Awards come around,
And the Oscar for Best Actor
in a Leading Role is given out,
I won't be shocked when I hear my name,
And start my acceptance speech
With thousands of Black people at my back,
Because all the world's a stage,
And no one has learnt how to act
Better than we have.

Botanical Latin

Non sunt in celi quia fuccant uuiuys Haitiansis Hochelaga
Translated:
They [the monks] are not in heaven because they fucked with the
Haitian wives of Hochelaga.

Niggers Are Scared of Paying Child Support

Niggers are scared of paying for child support, but niggers shouldn't be / scared of paying for child support, because child support is life support. / All niggers do is support being scared of paying for child support. / Niggers come home and hit my panties and leave change. Niggers change their / Heads from dreads, to Jheri-Curls opting for change. Niggers turn their / Backs on their own seed in the name of greed.

Niggers bullshit, talk shit, then hit leaving sistah's deranged. Niggers are Scared / of Revolution, the solution to my pollution. Niggers fuck! Niggers fuck, fuck, fuck! / Niggers love to fuck me, cos I'm sexy. Niggers vex me, thinking they're fucking / cute, hiding the loot, leaving black seeds while saying, "Fuck it! I did it!

Fuck you, screw you." Give niggers a little pussy and niggers say, "I Fucked you too." / Be a good woman to them, and they'll fuck you over! Fuck a four leaf clover, / fucking black queens around until their lives are over: Motherfuckers!

Niggers talk about fucking: Fucking that, fucking this, fucking yours, fucking my sis. / Not knowing that the sis they fuck becomes a nemesis when they duck. Give niggers fucking / love and devotion, as deep as the motherfucking ocean and they'll fucking drown / you in your own piss. Niggers fuck my thighs, your thighs, sci-fi's,and Mai-tai's, / give you a high-five, then fuck themselves from being fucking high.

Niggers would fuck fuck, if fuck could be fucked—my fucking luck! / But when it comes to paying for child support they say "Fuck you! I'm short. / My dick shall enter another port, fuck you and abort!" / Niggers are scared of paying for child support.

Niggers think they are fucking hardcore. Big boys trying to be men, / thinking that their dicks dictate the world, hard core niggers with a press and curl. Yeah, / Real fucking cute! When you hear niggers say "Baby, things are going to change!" / It means that niggers will knock you up and skip out on the small change. / It means they'll put their hands in your face if you wanna change. Change your tone of voice, change your life's choice, and they'll bring the pain. / The change you go through when you're black and blue will make you go insane.

Black Power! Black Power! Niggers piss on queens like a Golden Shower. / Beating on their woman means "Fight the Power." / Changes comes over them at night, in the darkest hour / as they sigh and moan: "White thighs, oh, white thighs," / when you know deep in your fucking soul that your thighs are black.

Too many niggers out there are smoking crack. Niggers do no' fucking love me, that's a fact. / Niggers are scared of paying for child support, but niggers shouldn't be / scared of paying for child support because child support is life support, / And all niggers do is support being scared of paying for child support.

EL JONES

Kings and Queens

This is for all my queens in Queens and all my kings in Kingston
raising a baby in Babylon.

If all of the sisters could fight for the brothers instead of fighting
over the brothers,
And all of the brothers could try to love their own instead of trying
to own love,
Then maybe we could fight like X did instead of fighting our exes.
And maybe if for a minute we stopped hating each other
We could do like Haiti and free each other.
And ladies—ask Harriet Tubman what it should mean to railroad each
  other
Instead of selling each other out we saw the soul in each other.
And brothers, we need to stop pimping Black women like we
learned from massa
And be more like Selassie instead of selling asses.

We used to go broke to go to school
Now we'd rather go broke than go to school
We were out in the hot fields dying to be cool
Now we're out in the streets dying to be cool
So we spend our last cent on those sweatshop shoes.
We take our government check but we don't check our government
We'll vote for American Idol but not the president
So while our brothers sit idle in Sing Sing
We don't care if our idols can sing sing.
And because we were sold to make sugar in Barbados and Bahamas
Now we talk about getting those sugar daddies and sugar mamas
And when we talk about dead presidents we mean cash and not Obama.

We're all up in each other's business but we can't get up in each
other's businesses
And then we wonder why we still don't own shit?
Instead of building like Egypt we try to "gyp" each other
And we'll rip each other off before we tip each other
And then we say, don't trip brother!
So we give each other props for still being property
And we fill our heads with hip hop but never with philosophy
While we buy anything unnecessary instead of by any means
necessary.

Black men call their home their crib
Like they're so busy being children they can't raise their kids
And they'll call their woman their babymama but never give her that ring.
We used to have to run away from the dogs so we could get married
Now we run away to be dogs instead of being called daddy.
And because we used to feel the crack of the whip
Now we sell crack to buy new whips
And instead of getting that diploma we'd rather dip.
So instead of working in that office and wearing a white collar
We get collared by white officers just to make that dollar
We want to play above the rim so we can buy new rims
Instead of taking engineering and building that pyramid.

We know everything about Judge Mathis
And nothing about what math is
We're so used to being money we've forgotten what cash is
And we can make that bank shot but we don't know where the bank is.
Because we're told we can play in the NBA but we can't be an MBA
And we can be an MC but not an MD or MA
And we don't talk about racism we just talk about playa hatin.
We dream about going to Liberia but we can't go to the library
So we're read our rights when we're sentenced instead of writing that
     sentence
We come from people who wrote the Book of the Dead!
Now we either end up booked or dead.

And maybe if we hung by our necks like our grandparents did
We wouldn't talk so hard about choking a bitch
And if we ever had to cut a lynching victim down we'd think twice
before we cut each other down to size
And maybe that's why we call each other shorty.

We talk about shooting each other with 9s and 45s
But we don't talk about working that 9 to 5
I guess we spent so long on the auction block
Now we'd rather die than get off the block.
So we end up on a chain gang in that jail
Cuz when we join that gang we can buy that chain
So we kill each other over shorting that weight
Just like massa did when he put cotton on the scale.

Ask a slave to show you a ho'.
Do you think he'd point at his sister in the next cotton row,
Or the tool in his hand used to make the cotton grow?
And when he sees the overseer coming ask him what it means to get low.
Ask him to point out free Black people I bet he'd never say BET
And brother, I don't think he'd say you
And sister, I don't think he'd say me.

IKENNA ONYEGBULA

Ethiopia

Speak to me of ancestry.

Drum your song of sorrow into my ears
and lynch my spirit upon the poetrees of your pain,
that I may hang upon each breath,
as I sway to the rhythm of your words.
Forget-me-not your memories as you present me with your history.
                                        Strike
familiar chords of anger inside my chest,
breaking my heart with the strength of the sorrow
                              of your beauty.

You,
who wallow in the heavens,
smiling devilish angelic
with cannons sewn into the sinews of your feet,
treading lightly on your pain for the sake of mankind,
for mankind has not always known how to Love you;
there is a goldmine laden with precious jewels
rumbling deep in the belly of your laughter—
a subwoofer in your larynx,
contracting a bass of sound in your vocal tract,
so swift, it carries with it enough holy strength
to decimate the earth.

                              You
hold civilizations captive
at the tip of your tongue—
—so speak
to me of ancestry,
because we have been much maligned,
but I refuse to believe that You
are nothing less than Divinity.

                              You
are pitch perfect heart-beat: electric,
rhythm and blues lungs

break-dancing to God's infinite human playlist,
equal tempo to the pulse of the Soul of the World,
and classically trained as a practising alchemist;
you
must be Negro;

yes, you
must be Negro,
but you are much more than an afro-funkadelic remixing
of the Holy Trinity of Love.

I
am from a land as ancient as thick thighs,
large hips, prominent breasts and slim waistlines,
mapping out contours of the immaculate conception of human
 civilization.
Long before Joseph Conrad peered into our heart of darkness,
ancient Nubian gods had been copulating with Mother Earth,
sprouting Love children of Ashanti and Kush tribes—
meandering across Egyptian state lines—
all the while inscribing the organic process of Black African rule
on papyrus leaves, poignant as hieroglyphs
etched into rock face.

So no, I can never be ashamed of who I be,
describe me as having the statuesque elegance
of dignitaries from Ancient Alexandria, going forward in time
and witnessing the carnage of modern day
war-torn Sierra Leone;
describe me as a cross between famine in Somalia
and the resilience it will take to bring relief home;
describe me as a revolt in Egypt and in Libya,
still fighting for the right to call my country my own;
describe me as rampant poverty;
but do it only so that you may call me bittersweet,
for I am also from a land of rich natural resources,
where the Kente cloth weaves a stunning romance
between the forest and the Savannah.

Momma,

look what they try to make me believe,
that my people are not enough;

        didn't you put these stardusts in our eyes
        and these war drums in our lungs?
        Don't we sound like a chorus of angels
        when we speak our native tongues?

Yet now, even decades after independence,
African skies still bleed rainbows of pain,
as I watch my Nigerian heritage washed away
by British colonial reign.
But no matter how you slice us, we are whole,
look through the windows to my soul and
you will come to know the true definition of a place
that I call home.

For Rome's ancient civilization ain't,
and never will have, a claim on our genetic throne,
because we now know no-body can pillage the natural resources
of our minds;
besides, I find that we are all African anyway,
children of ancient Ethiopia.
What do you know about Damot and the Kingdom of Axum
residing and thriving in Ancient Abyssinia?
Imagine
the heartbreaking beauty of splitting from an Atom,
entombed in the womb of mitochondrial Eve.

Speak to me of ancestry,
so that we
may entice our minds with higher discourses
and bask
        ·in the similarities …
of our souls!

JEN KUNLIRE

Climatic Interruption

A mouse spots crumbs on a tiled kitchen floor
Scurry, scurry, scurry
Teeny tiny rations served to chill
Private eye whispers "my love is near."
Lofty goals leave stale interpretations
Of the near-sightedness syndrome

Roaming fees increase

Deathly matters evoke territorial expansion
Handicap procedures dust the empty marginal lines
Fate claws at military war machines
An appetite used in biological warfare
Feared by Presidential leaks in up 'n coming scandals
Praised by mechanical scholars
Justified through acts of declaration and anti-rehabilitation
Levied prices prepare for the crash
Steamboats create dynasties below ocean deep cities
Buried underneath Atlantis
Forgotten like the Korean War

Justice is served on a silver platter
Better eat up before Africa starves; again
Another hungry child goes missing
Due to unexplained genetic experimentations
A willing specimen drawn in by breadcrumbs
Defeated by a mouse

Never leave the cheese behind an open door policy
It will only make matters unclear
And ultimately harder to fight for

GREG "RITALLIN" FRANKSON

Dear Shadow

dear Shadow,
i once used to wonder where the sun came from
how light illuminated our world
and allowed us to see
our surroundings, ourselves and each other,
marvelled at how water flowed through the stream
beside my Orton Park housing complex
and how the berries grew sweeter
than anything Highland Farms had on offer
in the produce section

dear Shadow,
i wanted to know why
the sun set on us before i knew
what one was to do with the light of dawn
why you melted away
like my Dickie Dee popsicle under the heat
of another Scarborough summer
leaving my hand empty, my mouth hungering
and a deep visceral thirst
unquenched by the passage of time and
the acts of imperfect mortal beings

dear Shadow,
bamboo shoots are versatile and strong
sugar cane sustains and timber
reinforces structures built on foundations
but all need to be cut down to size
in order to deliver their highly useful purposes
so it's difficult for me to compare you
to such crucial natural resources because
the sustenance you should have provided
blew away years ago like dust
from bamboo, cane and timber
burned away
from the cornerstones of my youth

there is no going back no turning back to back to back no i got your back
no back away from the flame son cuz it might burn you no i'll be right
back no back bacon cooking on the stove for me in the morning time
before school no back alley baseball games no backyard barbecues with
reggae rockers, red stripe and guinness no backing me up when i feel sad
or scared or alone no pats on the back for a job well done no grinning
face gazing at me with pride from the crowd no
no
no
no
no …

dear Shadow,
i'm now a grown man
with the power to express
what a child could only hem inside
the trauma of drama and psychoses
once held me prisoner to fear and regret
but i can't handle any more trials
so Guantanamo force-feed me
parables and platitudes
and excuses and equivocations
to satisfy my eternal curiosity
for there's no way my anger and fears
can subside as long as you
remain hidden beneath a cloud

dear Shadow,
you complicated matters
by setting up shop in East York—
a stone's throw away
from where my soul and flesh resided
and raised another seed
planted in the same season as mine, and you
sang to that seed and nurtured it, fed it and re-potted it
as it sprouted and matured under your watchful eye

even as i longed for a bit of that sun
that soil
that water
that comfort and joy

but Shadow,
the worst part for me is now
i am losing hold of the reality that once
fleetingly dominated my existence
and my nightmare scenario for my life
i sought to avoid all those years
takes root inside my tortured soul
why is it after all you've done to me
and all you haven't done for me, and
the pain i was exposed to long before my time
that your path is the one that illuminates itself
within the depths of the cave?

dear Shadow,
now i am a father too
i have my own seeds to nurture, feed, water and cherish
and having them live apart from me
hurts too much to think about too hard
so it scares me so much to know
that i have taken so much from you even when
you were not there to hand it to me in person

as i too melt away
and the sun sets
to leave no evidence of me
except for

a shadow.

NORDINE BEASON A.K.A. THE STORM

A Relaxed Chick

Cool like a snooze after eating chicken soup with dumpling
No-lye, napping dry to fry ends on temperature high
Prepping my hair to look super fly
To get first prize, a spot in your eye
Like a light-skin, tanned brown sugar delight
Every dark-skinned brother knows I'm right
As long as thick braids dangle from your cranium daily
Discounts don't happen for a dreadlock lady
Mayday! Mayday! I'm desperate for the "fit in" cream
The acceptable oil sheen extended dream
To smudge some self-esteem between each five minute comb-out hair
　　routine
Madly combing my hair during washroom breaks
When I should be near the pop machine, slithering words with office
　　snakes
Now, the hair fashion police officer is pissing me off
Because the media makes the dark feminine experience rough like a cough
Sister to sister … flip, flip, flip!
Hype Hair … flip, flip!
Black Hair, Styles and Care Guide … flip, flip, and flip!
Just flip through those issues and discover like an A&E lover
The greatest looks for "Difficult Hair" you suffer
Is compounded into letters and images to clutter your cynical self you
　　cover
Colours, colours, colours …
Cover girls and club girls enjoying the best
Trying to be like the rest
Maybe and maybe not, but you're it, and the style zone is hot
Tangle knots is what some of us got
Fresh party looks can put your savings three decimals left from the dot
But this insane check should jerk us back
For too much conditioning has been used on blacks
With silky chemicals penetrating ends when the perming process begins

Where is the means to our trends?
Where is the means to the split ends we bend?
There is a thin line below straightening systems that keep the hair frail
And damage roots like the perfection of a tight ponytail
Distracting your urges to scratch your hair anywhere
Worrying more, relaxing less when flakes are everywhere
So hail to the afro queens and beauty supply shops
With pin rolls, booming yaky and wigs by the dozen in stock
Never stopping the black women in getting what they want
To weave chunks of hair for the right to flaunt
But when I flip my hair to the side, the shallowness inside creates a shock
When I see a goddess walking self-confidently with her stream of
   dreadlocks!

BRANDON WINT

I May Never

I may never smell fresh cinnamon on an Indian woman's brown
   fingers
or see Guatemalan plums dangle like obsidian earrings on the lobes
   of rural trees.
Nor may I play voyeur to the sun when it hides coyly behind
   Kenyan mountains
but there are places I know where frost coats the inside of lungs,
and all of summer's hornets cannot sting so sharply as one invisible
   winter wind.

In this place, the moon is a dollop of pure honey
floating in black tea, and we watch our white breath rise
as the night steeps.

There may have never been hibiscus flowers parting their red lips
as I walked to school as a child
or mangoes dripping fragrance into my city streets
but on nights when I lay my body
against the calm, snowed earth
the crests of my flapping arms bring angels to the surface of the
   land.
There is a home for me between the magic and the struggle of each
   icy breath.

Though I may yearn for new places and new things
and my feet may call for new concrete
new muddied paths
new tones of brown from the bare flesh of the earth
no matter what freshness my senses crave
there will always be a familiarity in cold, naked trees
and the yearly martyrdom of fallen maple leaves.

There is even a place, a certain city
where I do not have to use my birth-name
because the streets have watched me grow.

The lowering sun has so often cast its glances through my bedroom
    window
The wind that shuttles between the narrow alleys could tell me
    stories
I've forgotten about myself.
It could sing the lullabies my mother used to sing.

Anyone who lives here could become the city's eyes
because we all know the red brick of the buildings.
We have all marvelled at summer's tulips
and the crackling colours of autumn's dying leaves
but only those who fill a place with their passion can become the
    city's heart.

I have given myself to the history of this place that has raised me
and it has returned to me the knowledge that all the exotic sands and
    shapes of the world
may be no greater a blessing to behold than the one pristine,
    unspoiled snowflake
balancing on my hot-blooded finger
in a place that is unmistakably my home.

AHMED KNOWMADIC ALI

Child Soldier

Before I could reach to pick up the soccer ball that had rolled under
the pick-up, I found myself peering
into the darkness of an AK barrel of a Somali kid I didn't know.
Forget what I looking for. Last thing I wish
to see is my soulless bloody body from a spirits perspective that is
no more. Little could I think, but I
must admit that I never thought that I would be belittled by a little
kid who knows little of what I did … to
him. I began to shiver as my sweat gathered mass like an avalanche,
time stood still, my body began to
chill and then began to tremble. My mind wandered searching for
and chasing dreams I let go years
before while it tries hard to assemble what values that I currently
resemble. Death excuses life and
welcomes regret and remorse as darkness begins to take its course.
But of course, like everyone about
to die I never loved long enough, deep enough, appreciated what I
had and stuff. But the African in me is
saying life is hard why complain be tough. So, I gather my
composure and get a little closer. He might be
a kid but it's for sure he's not a poser. My mouth gathers spit my
throat can't swallow, while I stare at
his eyes that are deep and hollow that made their home a mind that
is weak and shallow, with a record
of lives taken so I know I'm not mistaken to assume that if he kills
me, he will feel no sorrow. The tip of
the AK rests on my forehead, as he screams you're dead. I used
logic but he wasn't buying it because his
mind was too poor to afford it. Being it the reason why he had a gun
to make history and not a pen
to record it. Minutes have passed but I haven't passed I'm always
first for everything so I know I won't last.

Now I'm thinking, because it's all starting to sink in. You're already dead Ahmed, hit him with your right on
his chin and then follow through with its twin. Why today, why a kid of 14, why the first time back in
Somalia when I'm only 18. So many thoughts that they eventually become gridlock bumper to bumper in
my head like an American highway. Got me to thinking that if I had it my way, he would be pointing a
microphone in my face asking me what I thought about current issues in Somalia that day. Just a poor
skinny little kid with rags staring at me with bags under his eyes that sag, meanwhile unlike his
personality his brand new polished AK shines. I never thought light would hit me from the reflection of a
gun pointed by a kid who could have been my relatives' son. When I had given up and fear became
anger and frustration and I no longer had the patience I heard a voice say … "give him his ball we are
moving to the next location." He replied "I was just playing around with him I never had the temptation."
I got the ball back but I'm still searching for an explanation.

DAVID DELISCA

re(mind)her

It was right in the dead heat of winter.
Hot water decided not to
puff out its ring of steam through the showerhead's lungs.
So, it presented itself in a frosty zombified form.
Shit, I guess it just wanted to chill.
Had me thinking the last time this happened.
When we decided to boil the water
and steam up the washroom
by using the friction created by our bodies.
Washroom became the dressroom;
you wore me on you
and I wore myself on you.
Your flowing nectar of lava
plugged
between my rock and your soft place.
Really, I'm not thinking about you.

•

Went for a late-night grocery run.
The moon ate up the whole sky
just so
it could sit reclined in your passenger seat.
Reminded me how your soul ate up both my eyes;
your subtle urgent attempt to get next to me.
The only difference,
the moon doesn't touch a black man's radio
the way you would proudly do.
But really tho, I'm not thinking about you.

•

I was reading articles
and listening to the stories
that dripped off my ancestors' tongues
Tales about Hurricane Hazel wildly tucking
1000 Haitian lives and packing their spirits into the sky.
This was 1954.
Yet, you slithered across the floor of my mind.
See, all that needed to jump out was "…54"
Five-foot four, your height.
Just like the hurricane, in 3,2,1
the thought of you
wrapped around me with the strong wind eroding my heart.
Still, I'm not thinking about you

•

But do you,
think about me?

KHODI DILL

Ghost of Billie Holiday

This lady once told me that I was lucky, because black people don't age
And it's true that my grandmother bore the beauty of youth

But I wonder …
Do our faces not wrinkle because we bear the facelift of too much pulled
  hair?
Or because our expressions have been frozen with the shock of rape?
See at times at the altar
I fall and I wonder
How our bodies have been altered
By the passing of ships over bodies of water
By the lashing of whips over bodies of brothers

How our lips are enlarged from too many hits
Till they say we look like monkeys
Till they say we talk funny
But it's really because right here, education comes from money
So I diss the disproportionate spread of wealth
So I'm diabetic from the disproportionate spread of health
So the way I get rich is fist-over-hand
Clinging to ancestral ideals of wealth in distant lands
And it is true we must deal with the dealing of hands

Hands with white palms worn from all that Christian clapping
That once ran from Christians who were chasing and trapping
That once clung to a palm like life clings to a sapling
Hoping not to get taken
By the brand new colonial exploitation, exploration, domination—
subjugation—the commodifying, uninspiring anti-integration
Call me African-Canadian

See, my story lies in too many tombs
Where I have searched for my sons and daughters

My story lies in too many moonrises
Spent wading these cracked feet in water

Water, despite an old fear seated in muscles that recall a fall and a
   futile thrashing about
A fear seated in lungs that recall a last breath taken in terror and wet salt

My story lies in the brands blazed and the scars raised on my skin
   like a relief map
See they labelled me black and then they labelled my back
So everywhere I lie I leave a legacy of lines like a
        fingerprint

That's where my story resides
It's in those forty lines like forty acres I'm owed
Where forty trees might grow from the seeds that were sowed
My story is in hope
My story is a ghost of Kunta Kinte
My story is in the ghost of Billie Holiday

See my ancestors

       hang

from my family tree.

"Like strange fruit for the crows to pluck"
If Black people don't age, I wouldn't call it luck.

Patent Numbers II

To those names we forgot but whose life work lives on:

Swimming is refreshing & most love the water
But there was a time when many wouldn't bother.
Why you ask? I'm so glad you inquired,
Cause Sam Hines hadn't been inspired by a tire.
Saving lives was Sam's intention.
So naturally the life preserver was Sam's invention.
1, 13, 79, 71: Let's all pay respects to one of Atlantis' Sons.

From playing in the h2o to spraying it from plastic,
Lonnie G Johnson patented a classic.
45, 91, 071: May 27 '86—Water Gun

From having fun, to pooling blood on battlefields
What Clarence Gregg created had military appeal.
August 27, 1918
1st chilling sounds of the gun called machine.
12, 77, 307: Not only the patent but how many the "rat-tat-tat" sent to
  heaven.

Nathaniel Alexander in 1911 came up with a chair on July 7.
Initially intended for churches & schools
To accommodate people when they ran outta stools.
9-9-7, 108: Folding chair patent by Alexander the Great

Americans are patriots that's it there's no debating it.
In 1932 Francis Crighton found a place for it.
High above the heads swinging in the breeze
18-55-824: The flag pole displayed the flag with ease.

Bush man dem cook pon fia an' wood
But Lewis Dorcas thought this was no good.
Granted living in the south this was easier to manage
But Minnesota in October weather gets savage.
On the 10th 1907 Lewis had had it
Said "I need to be inside when boiling my cabbage."
Office gave its approval, iron box wooden fuel.
86, 84, 1-7: wood-burning stove, useful tool.

John Lee Love would sit at home alone,
Write & write & write to get the stresses off his dome.
A recurring problem the pencil would dull
& sharpening with a knife would make the knife blade null
59-91-14: From this clever carpenter; October 1897, pencil sharpener

Obviously not only brothers made a contribution
Sisters were right there keeping things moving
Sarah Boone for instance would never be called a pigeon
She patented an assistant to assist her fellow women
47-36-53: Sarah Boone 1892 ironing board

Lyda Newman had enough of fork & spoonin'
No more utensil usin' while doin' the head groomin'
Nov 15 1898 in a rush
61-43-35: Hair brush

April 1st, '87 Joan Clark made a start
To fashion an idea that came from the heart
That helped doctors & nurses in unprecedented ways
D28-32-49: Medical tray

So from nursing practitioners to folding chair creation
Don't get complacent, get an idea and face it
Make your dreams come true, cause that's what we do
Time to salute:
Patent numbers part II

KYM DOMINIQUE-FERGUSON

Call Me a Niggar

Call me a niggar!
I said call me a niggar!
I dare you to call me a niggar!

Called me Negro
meaning black
Negro rhyming with necro
Latin for death
so when massa raped our sisters,
mothers and daughters,
he was really expressing his inner necrophiliac!

Then after establishing the law
that one drop of black blood
makes you by default automatically black,
you want to separate us!
When your bastard sons
and daughters were born you'd say
"Now you'sa high coloured Negro,
and of the lot of them the prettiest and most presentable,
so i'sa gonna call you mulatto,
or my house Negro!
and you Jim Crow because
you'sa blacker than midnight and least like me,
you'sa field Negro or just my nigger"

That's whack!

Almost as whack as the red blue and white flag
waving in the sky,
when it should be red blue and black!
Built on the backs
of African slaves
screaming from their shallow graves
buried burnt
beneath weeping willow whispers of silent night,

deathly nights
there is no christmas for them.
They run through blood-soaked cotton fields
with apple trees bearing strange fruit,
under the blackest skies
with twinkling starlit night
and only the Moon Goddess as their guide.

Travelled in wooden boxes
living carcasses in a cheap sarcophagus,
unmummified they journey,
underground railroad travels
dangerous and perilous
massa always two steps behind
to Canada.
The land of the free.
Crying freedom,
Martin Luther Junior finding inspiration in the freedom reigning
but were they really free
or were they dumb,
were they free and dumb
making them free dumb
to the belligerent lies
of the Canadian veiled eyes,
settling squatters in unclaimed lands,
burrows like rodents assembling homes
creating the first
Afro-Canadian black community: Ville d'Afrique, Africville!

But where is it now on the map?
Search!
It doesn't exist.
Except in the memories of its poetry
and the descendants of Mister Mister Brown …
The first settler
of
Africville

You smile in my face
but you talk behind my back!
But what you lack,
is the facts!
You piss in the face of my history
Let your dogs shit in the spot my great-grandmother dug as a fire pit
to cook her seven kids a meal,
don't you fucking talk to me about equality
when the very same people
I pay my taxes to
are raping our his and her-story

So look me in the eye:
Call me a niggar!
I said call me a niggar!
I dare you to call me a niggar!

while your sleep is fitful i chant hellcat

caught in a storm between narcissism and neurosis,
i sat on the river's bank
and watched you
knee deep
while blue-grey silted water
enveloped your calves
sun shone off your pale chest
and
your hair crowned in flame

my european lover,
my black eyes cover you
curious about your exotic fantasies
of me
your chocolate piece,
your coño negra

does a part of your beautiful mind
believe
you own me
and
my s curves?
i inherited them from slaves
who once were
warriors who once
were goddesses
they will never
be yours,
of this i am sure

does your blood get hot with
colonial fire
when
i kneel before you
and let my tongue love?
my tongue that laps
can also lash
spit articulate fire on your polluted dreams,
and
did i mention
my
bite is worse
than my bark

i am no sensuous dog
but oh!
how i long to languish
near your legs
as i sit by the river's
edge.

MARLON WILSON

hip hop is

So I was just a youngsta when I worked for a Temp Agency
And I worked with a slimmy
I mean, a young white girl
She was hella fly
And the curves of her body undoubtedly caught my eye
She wore a baby blue Jump Man sweat suit
With a pair of mid-cut Jordan 13s to match
At the end of the work day to my delighted surprise
It would be the same bus we need to catch
Through gradual conversation
And our mutual flirtation
I found myself falling in love
Without the lust of penetration
I was so captivated by her artful language
And the anecdotal phrases that carried her thoughts
I swear someone could've yelled "the roof, the roof, the roof is on fire"
And we would intentionally miss our stop
After about an hour of our minds being locked
Without the gesture of a kiss
I ventured to ask her
What hip-hop songs would make your ultimate play list
Of course I'm guessing Nas "Rewind"
Or KRS-1's "Sound of the Police".
I mean a woman this refined
I could only be intrigued.
That's when she asked:

"You listen to hip-hop?
Don't you think it all pretty much sounds the same?
Bitch this, n-word that,
Spinning rims and flashy chains.
I guess I had you wrong
I thought you were a man of class.
How could you listen to music
That reduces women to a piece of ass?"

Hurt by her polarization
That attempted to define my very existence.
Because as intelligent as she was
She never took the time to listen.
Hip-hop is more than music,
Hip-hop is culture of the Big City Sound Girl
So marginalized by the mainstream
That in response she created her own world
That played by the rules
That a community would define
And with all due respect
You dress according to an identity
That a corporation has defined.
See you write off this music
As being shallow but if you dared to go deep.
You would drown in the similes, metaphors
And triple entendres that a group like Outkast would speak.

Hip-hop is a modern day negro spiritual
That is coded so Massah don't understand
Once you overstand that
Pick up some Mos Def and maybe some Sunz Of Man
Killah Priest, Immortal Technique, and Jean Grae.
I mean, how could you judge us
Off of what the radio plays.

The hip-hop you refer to
Is the blatant exploitation
Of poor people who act out modern day minstrels
In absolute desperation.
The wealthy have de-railed them
Social systems have failed them
And then when we require something to entertain us
That's when we play them.
You diss Waka Flaka Flame
Cause he rap with half a brain
But if he told you of his pain
Would you care to help him change?

Hip-hop is the voice of the children
Who no one gives a damn about in the streets of Palestine
Who instead of blowing themselves up as a battle cry
Pen first person accounts of the Gaza Strip battle lines.

You don't listen to hip-hop?
Who would've thought you'd be the same
As those who prejudge our culture,
As spinning rims and flashy chains.
I guess I had you wrong
I thought you were a woman of class.
Who would wait to form an opinion
After having all the facts.

BERCHAM RICHARDS A.K.A. DIRT GRITIE

Death by Consumption

I'm seeing how the game is played
A snake will eat his own ass to connect the chain
Each link off our wrist it's on our brain
Cause everything is consumer based
Free masons graduate to become Illuminati
The black market rules the world
You could ask John Gotti
Cause everything is consumer based

It's hard to conserve when they say spending
Is the only way they see this recession ending
Meanwhile the household debt
Is breaking the back
Of a fetus in the nut sack
Of some kid who ain't been born yet
So they say save
Yet hire sociologist to study our ways
The corporation
Will decide what you wear today
Cause everything is consumer based

The more we consume the more we waste
The more oil spills destroying lakes
The more carbon monoxide
Less air to breathe
Such an efficient killing machine
We did create
It's animals we fear but ourselves we hate
So much so
We would rather die than change
Cause everything is consumer based

Who do they ask when they pass bylaws
Putting restriction on product
I spent good money for
I spent too much time and energy

Putting myself in debt
Just to have things I haven't finish paying for yet
Cause everything is consumer based

Mommy you got makeup on at such a young age
Shallow eyes in a drawn on face
A white girl who fake and bakes
A black girl who bleaches
Only to find their features ugly
When sitting next to Beyoncé
Cause everything is consumer based

Selling me on the latest video game
Or dog did you see my new MJ's?
Damn ...
Understand, I'm not a business man
I'm a business, man
So buy into me
But you'll never own a part of my dynasty
I got a God complex
This is what concentrated wealth has given me
Everybody sing with me
H to the is O, V to the is A
Is it Jay-Z, Jahova, Jesus
Sounds strange?
Cause everything is consumer based

Well supply and demand
I demand we wage war
Cause I don't want pesticides
In my food no more
And even though I have the power
I set my sword to lay
Neglecting my ability to make change
Even though I know 2 elections take place
I refuse to vote with my dollars
But put an X by the name
Of a man who could care less
About where some kids play
Won't even take the time to explain
Why education's in decay
But when I vote with my dollars
That's when they get afraid
Cause they know
Like I know
And you now know
Everything is consumer based

SHARON WELCH

Our Sons

Our sons were never meant to wander in circles like Israel,
searching for the promised land.

Our sons were never meant to kill and rape each other by using
their tongue or putting a gun in their hand.

Our sons are born little boys who will grow up to be men.
Our sons are men, who are scared little boys that never mature within.

Our sons are lovers, dreamers, writers and then again.
Our sons are haters, blind, liars and desperately alone and never free men.

In prison, in the courts, on the streets, our sons are behind bars in
mental and emotional slavery.

Our sons are trapped in a worldly kind of shame. Our sons have
been lied to and told "Life is not a game." Oh but in life there are
winners and losers, throw a dice, a game of chance. Our sons have
lost hope, are deaf to the music, no one taught them how to dance.

Our sons are to be more than conquerors, world changers, and full
of destiny. But what does all this really mean?

The truth is, in God's eyes Our Sons are to be protected, nourished
and fed. It is only then they can truly be free.

GREG BIRKETT

The Race

Many were born ready but yet, forget to get set and go
Down in the starting blocks of life our reaction to the gun seems slow
We hear the bang, see the smoke but instead of going for broke we choke

As the human race starts without us,
we sit back quarrel, complain and cuss
and in refrain discuss how
Them cats got off to a better start than me,
they got two parents, all I got at home is moms and me,
and all the problems we see in a day, they wouldn't see in a year
Yo dis' race can't be fair!
How come my hurdles look higher than theirs?
I been training on Metro Housing stairs
While their plush facilities enhance their agility and upward mobility
Leaving me gasping for air
Running my laps in despair
Hoping those gaps disappear between me and my closest competitor

Maybe he'll be a doctor or a newspaper editor
But as for me yo, I don't know bout all that, 'cus
Math is hard still, and reading's kinda wack
So I'll just stay back, chill wid my peoples and have fun
Only time I'll move is when Sean Paul says fe "Give dem a run"[1]
Problem with that Black is you won't stay forever young
And sure as the rising sun you'll regret some things you've done

So my advice is quite precise and it starts with Step One,
Keep ya eyes on the prize, never sellout or compromise, be humble and
wise,
the man who always fails never tries

Step Two, I need y'all to be careful of who's runnin' with you,
'cus if they ain't positive you need to sprint and leave your crew
Now Step Three, avoid the approach of a coach named Jealousy and a
trainer named Envy as they pretend to be giving you tips to defeat your
enemies

In the end you'll see the energy it takes to hate
will make waste, and not haste
and time waits for no man,
Fast or slow man, so now I hand the baton to you
See, this race is a relay and someday you can teach your seeds what to do
True, there's a thirst for first, but speed and greed won't help you take the
lead
It's endurance and stamina that separates pros from amateurs, and
determines who succeeds.

EDDY GARNIER

Haïti Sees All Black [1]

Haïti is my misery
Let me sing my misery
I want to rap it even though it's no longer my poetry
I want to slam it even though it's no longer the song of my youth
I want you to know that I have a dream
A heavy dream an enduring dream an impossible dream
My dream
I invite you to dream it with me in my heart
Dream!

Haïti does not need a president
Haïti is sick
She requires doctors and rest
She has no democratic roots
It takes too much time to learn
After her recovery we'll put her to work
Haïti has no need for government
Parliamentarians spend their time blabbering
Haïti has no need for political candidates
They are candidates only to fund their retirement
The constitution was unable to prevent them
Haïti does not need elections
Since there is no need for a president
Haïti has just one program already planned: Reconstruction
Does any politician have a better plan?
Haïti requires temporary free zones
Administered by other nations (There's no charge, my dear)
Haïti requires municipal administrative councils
To oversee projects both local and national
Haïti requires quality control inspectors and program monitors
Haïti requires well-planned budgets

The politics of Haïti—will it be a history of never-ending beginnings?
Alas, it seems to be so.

A question of who you know, who's in charge, knowing the rules of the
  game.
A question of personal egos, a question of Self-Realization, a
question of abusers,
profiteers, etc.
Whereas in civilized countries, even if there are professional swindlers,
COMPETENCE, KNOWLEDGE, EDUCATION, COORDINATION,
PLANNING AND ORGANIZATION ARE PREREQUISITES
TO EVERY PUBLIC ACT, BRINGING INTO PLAY THE FUTURE
OF THE NATION AND ALL ITS INTERNATIONAL RELATIONS.

Alas! Alas and Alas! What a curse for all this time
Sa nou pat fè nap péyé - Haïti yo météw chita pou dòmi san rété!
From where comes this curse that's eating away at you, my love?

In this situation where you find yourself, dear country of Haïti,
elections should not even be considered since no candidate should
have any program in mind other than the one to rebuild the country.

It is the only dream worth having.

No matter who is elected, concentrate on just one program:
  Reconstruction.
In the six months following the earthquake, not one politician
has come forward with a plan, with ideas
Or even to suggest resources to mitigate the emergency that persists
and will endure
who knows how many decades to come ...

WHAT WILL THEY PROPOSE TO GET THEMSELVES
ELECTED TO THE PRESIDENCY OF THIS FINISHED
COUNTRY? That is the question? That is the question?
That is the question? Always the question. The same question.
Always! Always!
Always!
Why?

WHAT COULD A NEW CANDIDATE PROPOSE THAT ANY
OTHER WOULD NOT HAVE AS PRIORITIES FOR THE NEXT
30 YEARS, FOR THIS COUNTRY?

For this country there is no beauty in dying. No need for a president.
It is through the
exercise of a strong and articulate opposition that one recognizes a
candidate's ability to lead a nation.
There has never been one …
It's sad to say but you can't have an omelette without breaking a few
eggs.

IT'S LUCKY THAT THE EARTHQUAKE AND NATURAL
DISEASE CUT DOWN A FEW OF THESE UNCONSCIONABLE
UNCARING OBSCURANTISTS WHO
are blocking the natural political progress of this nation.
Yes the damn Constitution a leech Our leech constitution,
constitution of What?
In emergencies, this question of constitution, of the nationality of
this one or that one
is secondary.
Bato a ap koulé, le bateau coule sauve qui peut mézanmi, louvri jé
nou ! Li fin koulé.
The boat is sinking and it's every man for himself.

HAITI DOES NOT NEED ELECTIONS, SHE HAS NO NEED
FOR A PRESIDENT
right now. She does need a well-defined program of reconstruction,
with balance sheets, with project managers, with financing clearly
earmarked:
Roads, bridges, hospitals, schools, universities, irrigation, drinking
water, sewage systems, sustainable environmental programs,
REFORESTATION, REFORESTATION, REFORESTATION …
Clean-up, decentralization, dispersal, an articulated economic
  system based on
credit (as such the creation of jobs becomes a necessity) …

And not a system based on saving which slows economic progress
(there are
no jobs) …

Haïti is a nation (island) of winds, of sea, of sunshine, creators of
energies.

Why are there no wind power stations, solar power stations, ferries
to connect coastal
regions with larger centres?
Why is there no merchant fleet to facilitate commerce with the other
islands that sell
Haïtian artisan products in their own name?
My country does not need a president
My country does not need elections
Haïti has just one program already planned: Reconstruction
Does any politician have a better plan? Who? Who? Who?
Well then my God

WHAT CRIME HAVE WE NOT COMMITTED THAT WE ARE
PAYING FOR—HAITI YOU HAVE BEEN MADE TO SIT SO
THAT YOU SLEEP ENDLESSLY.

    THE BOAT IS SINKING, the boat is sinking every man for
himself MY
    FRIENDS, OPEN YOUR EYES, THE BOAT HAS SUNK.

Translated by Bruce Strand

JILLIAN CHRISTMAS

Fire

I do not need to tell you that you are enough,
You already know that everything that you are is all that you need.
Even though the weight of this world
Might sometimes bring you down to your knees
You must believe.
The poet Rumi once said
"What do you know of your yet undiscovered beauty?
One of these days, you will rise from within yourself like a sun."
So I offer you these words from my own heart, lips and tongue:
If you look around you, and everything is burning,
Licked in flames up-reaching like a funeral pyre,
Check if you are breathing.
If you are, it stands to reason,
That perhaps you're not the kindling,
You're the fire.

ANTHONY BANSFIELD

I am the Black Hockey Player

I am the Black Hockey Player
A brother who stands out on white ice like a fly in a pail of milk
Compose my surface smooth as silk
Cool like the ice I glide
Keep my anger on the inside
When the stands spit slurs
That echo like gunshots, or slapshots off the boards with the force in
their words
I'm like "Gimme the puck!" I don't give a ___ !
I know off the ice they pull you over for driving while Black
Sit your ass in the penalty box for that, doing overtime
Contemplating sudden death, yelling "Don't shoot!" while they take aim
As if to take away your last breath, all tangled up in their net
Easily identified, even behind the white wire of a goalie mask
So I play the game mentally and physically braced for impact, see
I am the Black Hockey Player.

I am the Black Hockey Player
I played through the cheap shots and chipped teeth
Stick slash and broke knee
I'm a throwback to guys like Carnegie and Willie O'Ree
Marson, McKegney, or Fuhr with the Fury
Even on blades, I blind you with the speed of an Anson Carter or Mike
  Greer
With the resilience built over 400 years
You could club me like Brashear
But still I persevere, after all
I am the Black Hockey Player.

I am the Black Hockey Player
Don't player hate me, I'm a pioneer
I'm like Henson at the Pole, out in the rink in the blistering cold
Forty below, freezing off my ears
The sole brown face
In places where they never seen, only heard rumours about my race
Afro puffing out the sides of my helmet
Body check
Why do I get extra attention from the ref?
Never picked for the top teams no matter how good I get

I am as rare as brothers in the Winter Olympics!
I am absent from the Hall of Fame, or the All-Star game
Even Black history experts don't know my name
All the same, I walk softly but carry a big stick
Got visions of drinking Baby Duck from the Stanley Cup
With an all-Black starting line-up
While the P.A. system play some funk
Like Kool and the Gang to celebrate my rising star
I'll have some folks turning the channel to NASCAR as their last
sports bastion
Now that the Williams sisters and Tiger took over
Their country club games as champions
And so will I, and do you know why? Cuz
I am the Black Hockey Player.

I am the Black Hockey Player
I am playing in a league where the idea of equality is bush league
Where it's like the era of Jackie Robinson, for me, the Black
Hockey Player
They're saying I don't have a prayer
Like the way the way they declared a Negro can't survive in the cold
up there
Only good for serving as porters on their trains up there
Or working as domestics in their big homes up there
But now we deep in the city
Like the Capital, where winter hits with no pity
Or in Montreal where I twice saw the whole place mash up in a riot
Just cuz their team won it all, people all drunk and wild
And from when I was a child, I had heroes like Dr. J, but also Yvan
Cournoyer
I loved my trading card of Willie Mays, but also my Jean-Claude
Tremblay
I got chills down my spine when I heard the call and response
Of the crowd and organ play:
Dooh-dooh-dooh DOOT-dooh-DOOH …
CHARGE!!!

Wanted to hear the crowd cheer for me, too
But all they did was call me Nigger and boo
And urge their sons to beat me black and blue
When all I wanted was to wear my team's colours
The bleu, blanc et rouge
I am the Black Hockey Player.

I am the Black Hockey Player
But my Pops love a game a cricket,
Talking fast bowler and wickets
Taught me how to play the real football, and
Took me back to Iere so I could feel at home under palms
All the same, I could thrive in ice storms, and snow squalls
As comfortable cradling black rubber as a ball
Style like Pele on a breakaway
Amazed the skeptics who said I couldn't make the grade
Bounced from team to team in the minors to try and ply my trade
I tried out for the Rangers, but they treated me like a stranger
Stagnated, low-rated, my career was in danger
So I was traded, went from the frying pan to the fire
Found myself riding the bench for the Flyers
Released and picked up on waivers by the Canucks
Then I found out the coach was a closet Ku Klux
We got on like Spree and Carlissimo
Blackballed, blacklisted, my future looked "abysmal"
I think it's criminal, but I have defined a new mission
To tell the world my story, communicate my vision
To the next generation, tell them to keep going, like Jesse Owens
Scorned, but reborn in a million youth marching to carry on
So that one day, they can say with less anger in their eyes than I
When I say once again that
I am the Black Hockey Player.

A Note on Black Canadian Poetry

A Note on Black Canadian Poetry

"We must understand that we are creating, for instance, an African Canadian literature, one that is a branch of Canadian literature, but which also maintains definable, Africanist oral/linguistic strategies, as well as a special relationship to song, rhythm, and a specific history." [1]

The Great Black North is a land where identity is created as much as it is inherited. This anthology is an effort to recognize the poetic traditions of peoples of African descent in Canada as well as establish a new tradition for the spoken word generation of wordsmiths, dub poets, lyricists, emcees, performance poets, and slammers who have been performing their orature at the highest levels locally, regionally, provincially, nationally and on international stages.

I attended my first poetry slam in 2002. By 2004, I had composed my version of the definitive Black History Month poem—a poem written with the intention of performance. I performed my words at the Vancouver Poetry Slam Black History event with Dwayne Morgan as the feature poet. This attempt to define myself and my story with the spoken word came at a time in my life when graduation from university, marginalization from my profession and global awareness were fresh-spoken experiments to be shared. The results of testing the poetic waters were refreshing and were anthologized in *We Have A Voice: African & Caribbean Student Writing in B.C.* At a slam, it is the people who decide what they like, and the popularity of this contemporary phenomenon is partly due to its accessibility from a broad range of oral expressions. In addition to the aforementioned spoken word generation, there are ranters, ravers, actors, comedians, musicians and page poets found at poetry slams or on the open mic that precedes many of them. However, many contemporary spoken word artists choose to present their work outside the competitive venues of slam poetry. When I met Tanya Evanson at the slam, she invited me to perform at her event *Under the Griot Tree*. I felt a familial resonance that accompanied me with music as I presented my poetry with a band aptly named *African Science*. In other words, I was introduced to the sound and power of the spoken world once I started to use my voice.

Similar to Evanson, I had grown up in a Canadian environment but with a Caribbean foundation. I have fond memories of my mother teaching with the poetry of Miss Lou, emphasizing the folklore, language and culture of Jamaica. Just as her poem *Antigua, Antigua* uses repetition in the same way that Damian "Jr. Gong" Marley pays homage to his island homeland in *Welcome to Jamrock*, it also refers to Canada when she contrasts the hot Caribbean sun with the cold northern ice formations and mentions "me nah Gretzky." Although I grew up watching "The Great One" lead the Edmonton Oilers to four Stanley Cups, I feel her on the sentiment that hockey is a product of the northern climate zone, unfamiliar to most newcomers from temperate equatorial regions, yet it is still connected to the history of the Black community in Canada.

> *"The right storyteller protected the laws, the secrets and the culture of the community which would enable the people to understand both their natural and supernatural world. And so it became that the role of the storyteller and the role of the writer were both powerful and awesome."* [2]

African-Canadian literature and orature are explorations of rhythm and region in a multicultural context. It should be noted that the term African Canadian, according to George Elliott Clarke, refers to persons and expressive cultures located in or derived from Canada, possessing to some degree an ancestral connection to sub-Saharan Africa. The phrase encompasses, then, recent immigrants to Canada from the United States, the Caribbean, South America and Africa itself, as well as the indigenous, Africa-descended community. As Karina Vernon emphasizes in her preface to this volume, a defining point of Black Canadian poetry is that it is not only found on the page, but is often vocalized and performed on stage. This practice of the oral tradition is empowering because it is a spiritual discipline that synchronizes the life the poet leads with the words that they speak.

An annual gathering place for the spoken word generation of performance poets is the Canadian Festival of Spoken Word. At my first CFSW in Halifax in 2007, I witnessed first hand the living history, controversy and diversity of the Canadian family from coast to coast. But what I remember the most was the "Afros Only" photo taken on the last night of the festival in a spontaneous show of Blackness and solidarity in a space where *Word Iz Bond* is both a collective and a philosophy. By 2010, the festival was in Ottawa, the original launching point for the annual celebration of spoken word arts and the Canadian national poetry slam competition. As national politics in the spoken word family started to resemble the discriminatory constructs of the society that we often speak out against, I was compelled to facilitate a *Spoken Wordshop* based on the idea of the oral treaty that poets bind themselves with and the responsibility that comes with the words we "spit."

> *Spit not in the wind.*
> *Be not too proud to spit your truth out loud.*
> *As a man thinketh, so too he spitteth.*

Spit not, lest ye be spit upon.
The best spitter is a better listener.
Actions spit harder than words.
A word spat is a bond intact.

- Scruffmouth, "Seven Laws of Spit"

My connection to this network of "Northern Griots" was like discovering my superpowers and joining a team of likeminded individuals each with their own skill set but sharing a common goal and a methodology by which to achieve it. When I was invited by Valerie Mason-John to work on this anthology, I gladly accepted the opportunity to co-edit this timely publication. It was a chance to learn as much as I could about the established, intermediate and emerging Canadian poets of African descent and connect the dots between genres and generations. I appreciate the work that has been done by individuals such as Anthony Bansfield and others involved in the *Northern Griot Network* as they paved a trail for many of us to walk and talk on. Much like the challenges faced by "The Black Hockey Player", struggle and sacrifice are also common themes in our lives. As a listener and a reader, I am continually inspired by fellow poets, colleagues, elders, ancestors and youth.

This anthology is an effort to select the right storytellers to answer the question: What is Black Canadian poetry? There is a defining feature in many of the poems found in this anthology: a reaffirming signification of identity and ethnic origins found in content, prose and genre. This "patchwork quilt of voices" keeps us warm as we share our stories "on the fringe of diaspora." It would seem that the thread binding the quilt is Canadian, though the style in which the pattern is woven is a memory of Africa. This inheritance is alluded to in Bertrand Bickersteth's poem "We, Too" as he pays homage to the renowned American poet Langston Hughes. Aside from drawing on cultural and artistic influences from our American neighbours, we also share social and political similarities such as the phenomenon of slavery, which is largely ignored in the Canadian mainstream but acknowledged in America as a fundamental institution. Therefore, we see Afua Cooper on double assignment as historian and poet as she recalls these tales in "Confessions of a Woman Who Burnt Down a Town" based on the last days of Marie Joseph—an enslaved African in New France. As storytellers, we have an obligation to shed light on the past so we can see our future.

Use this book to keep you warm with its contrasting fabrics of print poetry in the page section and performance poetry in the stage section. Within each genre is a multicultural display of knowledge and insight that should serve as ample insulation in the cold Canadian winters. There area the historical descriptive narratives of scholars, the insightful observations of neighbourhoods and families, the riddims and revelations of dubpoets, the social commentary of spoken word, the identity, impact and immediacy of slam poetry. Each poem contains stylistic elements that combine to form a more complete picture of what Black Canadian poetry is. As the reader, you are integral to the function of this anthology like audience members participating in live performance. Thank you.

> *"Black writers honour the link between being and language, between empowerment and articulation. They cannot cease to do so. The word is out."* [3]

Kevan Anthony Cameron, July 2012

Notes and Biographies

Notes and Sources

Page

p. 27 In June 1734 Marie-Joseph Angélique, a Black slave woman, was hanged in Montreal for burning down much of the town that April. Her last days provide the inspiration for this poem.

p. 75 "legba" is in reference to the gate-keeper lwa of vodou that allows for passage between the material and spiritual worlds.

p. 94 "duppies" are spirits or ghosts in the Jamaican vernacular.

p. 98 "crapaud" is the frog, the most detested creature on the island. Often poisonous, they are hated worse than snakes.

Stage

p. 109 "Oonu" is all of us, all of you, all of we, in the Jamaican vernacular (patois).

p. 156 "A Fly in a Pail of Milk" is an allusion to the Herb Carnegie story of the same name.

p. 241 "give dem a run" is a reference to a dance made popular by the Jamaican dancehall icon Bogle. From the song "Like Glue" by Sean Paul.

p. 243 "Haiti Voit Tout Noir" by Eddy Garnier. Translated from the French by Bruce Strand.

A Note on Black Canadian Poetry

[1] *Odysseys Home: Mapping African-Canadian Literature.* George Elliott Clarke. University of Toronto Press Inc. 2002. p. 203

[2] *Daughters of the Sun, Women of the Moon: Poetry by Black Canadian Women.* Edited by Ann Wallace. Williams-Wallace Publishers. Stratford, Ontario. 1991. p. 6

[3] *Odysseys Home: Mapping African-Canadian Literature.* George Elliott Clarke. University of Toronto Press Inc. 2002. p. 276

Bibliography to *A Note on Black Canadian Poetry*

Daughters of the Sun, Women of the Moon: Poetry by Black Canadian Women. Edited by Ann Wallace. Williams-Wallace Publishers. Stratford, Ontario. 1991.

Eyeing the North Star: Direction in African-Canadian Literature. Edited by George Elliott Clarke. McClelland & Stewart Inc. Toronto. 1997.

"I am a voice crying in the wilderness, on the fringe of diaspora." – Carol Talbot.

Fiery Spirits & Voices: Canadian Writers of African Descent. Edited by Ayanna Black. Harper Collins Publishers Ltd. 2000.

Odysseys Home: Mapping African-Canadian Literature. George Elliott Clarke. University of Toronto Press Inc. 2002.

Heart of a Poet. TV series. *http://www.heartofapoet.ca/*

Our Souls Have Grown Deep Like The Rivers: Black Poets Read Their Work. Rebekah Presson Mosby.

On Imagination "There in one view we grasp the mighty whole,/ Or with new worlds amaze the unbounded soul." – Phyllis Wheatley.

Orality in Writing: Its Cultural and Political Function in Anglophone African, African-Caribbean, and African-Canadian Poetry. Yaw Adu-Gyamfi. Thesis Dissertation. University of Saskatchewan. *http://digitalcommons.liberty.edu/fac_dis/83/*

Oxford American Writer's Thesaurus, second edition. Christine A. Lindberg, Oxford University Press Inc. 2008.

Revival: An Anthology of Black Canadian Writing. Edited by Donna Bailey Nurse. McClelland & Stewart Ltd. 2006.

This is How We Flow: Rhythm in Black Cultures. Edited by Angela M.S. Nelson, University of South Carolina Press. 1999.

Biographies

Preface

Karina Vernon is Assistant Professor of English at the University of Toronto Scarborough, where she specializes in Canadian literature, black Canadian cultural studies, archives, and urban Canadian studies. She is co-founder and editor of Commodore Books, the first black press in Western Canada, and she is a member of the Hogan's Alley Memorial Club, a grassroots cultural organization dedicated to preserving the memory of Vancouver's historical black presence.

Exceptional Poetics

George Elliott Clarke (1960-) was born in Windsor, Nova Scotia. Still an "Africadian" landowner, he teaches at the University of Toronto. His honours include the Portia White Prize for Artistic Achievement (1998), Governor-General's Award for Poetry (2001), National Magazine Gold Medal for Poetry (2001), Dr. Martin Luther King Jr. Achievement Award (2004), Pierre Elliott Trudeau Fellowship Prize (2005-2008), Dartmouth Book Award for Fiction (2006), Poesis Premiul (2006, Romania), Eric Hoffer Book Award for Poetry (2009), appointment to the Order of Nova Scotia (2006), appointment to the Order of Canada at the rank of Officer (2008), and eight honorary doctorates.

Poets

Page numbers at end of biographies refer to contributors' poems.

Adelene da Soul Poet is who I be/I'm the descendent of the Black Pioneers/On Salt Spring Island B.C. / The matriarchs have instilled in me/The importance of my poetry/To keep our history alive! / Women we move forward with strength, pride and grace! *Page 178*

Ahmed "Knowmadic" Ali, an award-winning poet, is Albertan. Somali by blood and birth, he emigrated to Canada at the age of eight. Ahmed is a nationally recognized and respected poet who tours spreading his message. *Page 221*

John Andrew Omowole Akpata is a Spoken Word artist based in Ottawa, Canada. He has won many titles and awards, and has toured internationally. A man of Nigerian and Guyanese heritage, John represents a new generation of Canadian griots. *Page 143*

Lillian Allen is a leading international exponent of dub poetry hailing from Spanish Town, Jamaica and currently residing in Toronto as Professor of Creative Writing at the Ontario College of Art & Design University. Her latest CD (2012) is titled *Anxiety*. *Pages 108, 110*

Anthony Bansfield is African, Trinidadian, Breton, Taino / mixdown in Parry Sound and Ottawa, Ontario / heroes Irving and Anne-Marie, mentors Lillan and Kali / founded festivals and series with friends and colleagues / legacy like N'x Step, NorthCoast, WordLife, south-north griots. *Page 248*

Siobhan Barker, of Caribbean ancestry, hails from Southern Ontario, now living in B.C. by way of Quebec. She is a bilingual singer, storyteller, published fiction/non-fiction author, facilitator, and textile artist committed to responsible reconsumption. *www.putahaton.com* *Page 183*

Nordine Beason (The Storm) is a spoken word poet from Toronto, Canada. As a digital artist of Jamaican heritage, her performance poetry has been powered by her personal experiences and passionate heart. She has been published in the *Urbanology Magazine*. *Page 217*

Bertrand Bickersteth was born in Sierra Leone, raised in Canada, educated in the U.K. and, until recently, resident in the U.S. Having returned to Calgary, his work focuses on black identity in Alberta and was recently featured in *Abronet Magazine*. *Pages 68, 69*

Greg Birkett, a Torontonian, was a finalist for the Governor-General's Award for Excellence in Teaching in 2011. He co-authored the textbook *Black History: Africa, the Caribbean, and the Americas*. His play *Do You Remember Me* was featured in the 2012 Toronto Fringe Festival. *Page 241*

Juliane Okot Bitek is an award-winning writer, but no trophies for balancing family life & grad school. Born in Kenya to Ugandan exiles, she now lives in Vancouver, Canada where she writes, teaches and studies. *Page 43*

Charlie Bobus: International motivational dub poet, Nicardo "Charlie Bobus" Murray is a Jamaican based in Toronto. A multicultured performer/ youth activist of mixed race. Related to the Vernon family of Toronto. Released *Creative Energy* poetry book, album & video to much acclaim. *Page 138*

Shane Book's first collection, *Ceiling of Sticks*, won the Prairie Schooner Book Prize and the Great Lakes Colleges Association New Writers Award. He is a graduate of the Iowa Writers' Workshop and was a Wallace Stegner Fellow at Stanford University. *Page 38*

George Augusto Borden has lived in the Halifax-Dartmouth area of Nova Scotia since 1975. An African Nova Scotian of mixed racial heritage including Mi'maq and Dutch, his heritage in Canada goes back to the Black Loyalists arrival in 1783. *A Mighty Long Way! Page 45*

Wakefield Brewster is one of Canada's most dynamic performing Black poets. He was raised in Toronto and now lives in Calgary, Alberta, while performing frequently across North America. *Page 152*

Klyde Broox (a.k.a. Durm-I), internationally respected dub poet, has decades of performance experience in North America, Europe and the Caribbean. A consummate stage artist, he blends speech, song, dance and mime into a powerful package that is inspirational. *Page 113*

Brother Sankofa is Afrikan, Jamaican, committed, controversial, persistent and works as a poet, pan-afrikan radio programmer and community activist. Sankofa came to Ontario in 1987 from Jamaica and completed a full length album titled *Sankofa Ancestral Calling* in 2010. *Page 132*

Ryan Burke, author of "New World Diaspora Man", a poem released on a spoken word CD with other young Canadian poets, is a native of Toronto, Ontario. He is the only child of two West Indian parents and is a 1st generation Canadian. *Page 172*

Jillian Christmas was born in Markham, Ontario. She currently lives in Vancouver, B.C. where she serves as co-director of Verses Festival of Words. She facilitates youth programs across Canada and is a member at large of Spoken Word Canada. *Page 247*

George Elliott Clarke: G.E.C.'s poetry books in print: *Red* (2011), *I & I* (2009), *Blues and Bliss* (2008), *Trudeau* (2007), *Black* (2006), *Illuminated Verses* (2005), *Québécité* (2003), *Blue* (2001), *Execution Poems* (2000), *Beatrice Chancy* (1998), *Lush Dreams* (1994), and *Whylah Falls* (1990). *Page 32*

Wayde Compton's latest book, *After Canaan: Essays on Race, Writing, and Region* (Arsenal Pulp Press, 2010), was nominated for a City of Vancouver Book Award and was an iTunes Book of the Week. He lives in Vancouver. *Page 30*

Afua Cooper is the J.R.J. Chair in Black Canadian Studies at Dalhousie University. This scholar is a founder of dub poetry in Canada, publishing five books and recording two CDs. She won the Beacon of Freedom Award for her novel *My Name is Phillis Wheatley. Page 27.*

d'bi young. anitafrika, afrikan-jamaican-canadian dubpoet, monodramatist and educator, is the author of 4 books, 2 dub albums, and 8 plays. artistic director of the gurukul in kingston jamaica and originator of the sorplusi method. *sankofa* is her latest publication. *www.dbi333.com* *Pages 122, 125*

David Delisca Writer-performer David Delisca is a Haitian-born, Palm Beach, FL raised, Toronto resident. *Page 223*

Adebe DeRango-Adem is a writer and English Ph.D. candidate at the University of Pennsylvania. She is the author of the poetry collection *Ex Nihilo* (Frontenac House, 2010) and co-editor of *Other Tongues: Mixed-Race Women Speak Out* (Inanna Publications, 2010). *Pages 59. 60*

Khodi Dill, the son of a Bahamian mother and a Canadian father, is a spoken word poet, hip hop artist, and educator living in Saskatoon, Saskatchewan with his wife, Carly Brown. Several of Dill's poems and tracks are available online. *Page 225*

Osaze Dolabaille, author of *Rebirth of the Warrior Poet,* emigrated from Trinidad as a toddler. A childhood spent in urban southern Ontario led him to embrace Afrikan spirituality as an adult. This singer, drummer and poet now resides in Toronto. *Page 164*

Kym Dominique-Ferguson is Montreal born while raised in Jamaica and Haiti. His work draws on the past, present and the sciences. He currently produces 2 spoken word events in Montreal: a monthly Open Mic & an annual erotic poetry show. *Page 229*

Yvette Doucette After 13 years in Toronto, Ontario, poet Yvette Doucette is back on P.E.I. where she was born to her Jamaican mother and French father. Her work has been published in *Letting Go: An Anthology of Loss and Survival* and in *Arts East Online. Pages 129, 131*

Eddy Da Original One is an African-Canadian performance poet-beatboxer/storyteller, born in Ottawa, Canada, raised in the Caribbean island of Trinidad and Tobago, now residing in Toronto. His writings can be read in *T Dot Griots: An Anthology of Toronto's Black Storytellers. Page 184*

Nehal El-Hadi (Ontario/Saskatchewan) is a Sudanese-born writer, researcher and editor, whose work examines the interplays between the body, place and technology. She is the author of the chapbook *city/heart,* and is currently working on her first collection of poetry. *Page 187*

Tanya Evanson is Antiguan-Québécoise in B.C. Poet, Spoken Word Artist, Vocalist, Arts Organizer, Educator & Whirling Dervish, she is the new Director of Banff Spoken Word. "Language for Gods", her third album, was released autumn 2012. mothertonguemedia.com. *Pages 146, 147*

Rudyard Fearon was born in Jamaica. He works at University of Toronto Robarts Library. *Free Soil*, his first book, is published on CD-ROM with CD audio tracks. Rudyard is a poet profiled in the television series "Heart of a Poet". *www.rudyardfearon.com*. *Pages 83, 84*

Gregory Frankson a.k.a. Ritallin is a first-generation Jamaican-Canadian raised in Toronto, Ontario. A key contributor to the Canadian slam scene and author of *Cerebral Stimulation*, Greg is also the Poet Laureate of the International Initiative for Mental Health Leadership. *Page 214*

Michael Fraser was born in Grenada. His first poetry book, *The Serenity of Stone* (Bookland Press), was published in 2008. He won the Arc 2012 Readers' Choice Poem of the Year. He lives and teaches high school in Toronto. *Page 77*

Addena Sumter-Freitag, author of *Back in The Days,* is an award-winning author presently living in London, ON with her heart in Vancouver, B.C. She is 7th generation Black Canadian with family roots in Nova Scotia (and South Carolina). *Page 56*

Whitney French is a writer, educator and literacy advocate living in Toronto, Ontario. Born in Canada and raised by Jamaican parents, she has written poetry, fiction and articles professionally since 2008. Her book *3 Cities* was published in April 2012. *Page 86*

Eddy Garnier, born in Hinche, Haiti, became, by force of impromptu, a poet, novelist, short story writer, author of tales. He has written novels, poetry, monologue and other genres. A versatile and prolific artist, he touches on almost all areas of writing and the art of saying. *Page 243*

Melvina Germain: Diversity is the diamond chip of poetic success. Melvina Germain, born in Sydney, Nova Scotia validates and exemplifies that. Her perpetual passion and yen for broadening her literary scope has enabled her to establish herself as a solid multi-style poet. *Page 166*

Lorna Goodison is regarded as a major figure in world literature, and her eight books of poetry, a memoir and two collections of short stories have received much international acclaim. She teaches at the University of Michigan and lives with husband Ted Chamberlin in Halfmoon Bay, B.C. *Pages 46, 47*

Shauntay Grant is an award-winning writer and spoken word performer from Nova Scotia's historic Black community. She has performed internationally, served as Halifax's third Poet Laureate (2009–2011), and was a Poet of Honour, Canadian Festival of Spoken Word, 2010. *Pages 79, 80*

Sylvia D. Hamilton, multi-award-winning Nova Scotian filmmaker-writer, is a descendent of the Black Refugees of the War of 1812. Her films have been screened in Canada and abroad. Her most recent film is *The Little Black School House*. *Page 53, 55*

Claire Harris, a native of Trinidad, won the Stephansson Award several times. *The Women's Quarters* won the 1984 Commonwealth Prize for Poetry, Americas Region; *Drawing Down a Daughter* was nominated for the 1992 Governor General's Award and the F.G. Bressani Prize. *Page 119*

Amy Marie Haynes' poems are born in moments of exultation. some get written down, some are shared. others just swirl around inside as inspiration for her endless questions, moisture for her thirsty soul, and material for a mind wont to dream. *Page 232*

Harold Head: I was born in South Africa where I was an apartheid journalist. Compelled to leave in 1964, I entered the U.S. for study. When I arrived in Canada in 1973, with the support of the U.N. Association (Toronto), I produced Athol Fugard's play "Boesman and Lena" to mark the Sharpeville (S.A.) massacre of 1960. I published a chapbook titled *Bushman's Brew* and in 1976 the anthology *Canada in Us Now*. *Page 100*

Jemeni is an award-winning poet based in Toronto. Born in the Island of Grenada, she immigrated to Canada as a child. Her CD *Feature Trippin* is a collection of spoken word collaborations with artists from all around the world. *Page 159*

El Jones, spoken word activist and teacher, was captain of the two-time National Champion Hali slam team and has performed across Canada. She teaches in Women and Gender studies at Acadia university and in the African Canadian Transition Program at Nova Scotia Community College. *Page 207*

Reed "iZrEAL" Jones is a Toronto-born writer and director raised in the African Nova Scotian community of Upper Hammonds Plains. He is a national slam champion and represented Canada at the World Cup of Poetry in Bobigny, France. *Pages 148*

Anthony Joyette is a naturalized Canadian painter and poet of Caribbean origins (St.Vincent and the Grenadines). He lives in Quebec and is a founder of *KOLA*, a Black literary magazine. His most recent book is *For Judas Iscariot in Heaven and other poems*. *Page 58*

Ian Kamau: My name is Ian Kamau; I am an artist. I was raised in Toronto to filmmaker parents who came from Trinidad in 1970. I believe in community. My creative life actively involves my community work. I write, I make music. *Page 189*

Dr. Naila Keleta-Mae, artist-scholar, is Assistant Professor in the Department of Drama and Speech Communication, University of Waterloo. Second generation Canadian of Jamaican descent she has numerous published poems, two albums, three plays and one experimental performance installation. *www.nailakeletamae.com*. *Page 191*

Ian Keteku was born to Ghanaian immigrants living in Alberta. Currently residing in Ontario, Ian is an acclaimed artist and 2010 World Poetry Slam Champion. Ian recently released his debut spoken word album *Lessons From Planet Earth* (Re-Evolution). *Page 197*

Jen Kunlire, second generation Jamaican and Nigerian, is a Calgary native spoken word poet. Her work has appeared on the CBC, she has written 6 chapbooks and was titled the People's Poetry Festival Poet of Honour in Calgary. *Page 213*

Robert Layne: My name is Robert Layne a.k.a. Markus Black, The Only Good Negro. I hail from St. Vincent and the Grenadines and came to Canada in the early 90s, now residing in Hamilton, Ontario. My background and love is Blackness. *Pages 127, 128*

Marva Jackson Lord was born in Jamaica and raised in Goderich, Ontario. A proud Black Canadian rooted in African, Celt, Scottish Jewish, Native Caribbean and Chinese bloodlines, she is now based in the Black Mountains of Wales, happily scribbling away. *Page 94*

Jean Pierre Makosso, bilingual storyteller in Gibsons, B.C., is from a traditional background. Originally from Congo Brazzaville, and taught by his mother Ma M'Kayi, when enrolled in the Occidental school system he displayed his taste for words and verbs. His latest book is *Human Works.* *Page 193*

ahdri zhina mandiela, of Jamaican origin, is founder and artistic director of a Toronto-based performance company, *b current*. She is best known as a poet/performer. Her art materials include published works, CD recordings, dance choreographies, and video projects. *Page 41*

Suzette Mayr, born and raised in Calgary, Alberta, is part German, part Bahamian, with a bit of Caribbean Scottish thrown in. Her most recent novel, *Monoceros,* won the W.O. Mitchell Book Prize and was longlisted for the Giller Prize. *Pages 39, 40*

Ashley Alexis McFarlane is a poet, fashion designer, filmmaker and photographer of Jamaican Maroon descent. She was born in Toronto and creates art inspired by her African ancestry, spirituality, and mother nature. For more info visit her blog. *www.asikereafana.com* *Page 176*

Pamela "Pam" Mordecai, award-winning poet of West African, Asian and European heritage, has lived in Ontario since emigrating from Jamaica in 1994. Well-known internationally for her children's poetry, she writes across genres. TSAR published her fifth poetry collection, *Subversive Sonnets* (2012). *Page 88*

Dwayne Morgan is a first-generation Canadian of Jamaican heritage. Morgan has had six volumes of his poetry published, most recently *Her Favourite Shoes* (2011), following his first translated work, *Le Making of d'un Homme*. *Page 200*

Motion is a poet/emcee and playwright whose work fuses the realms of music, spoken word & drama. Born & raised in Toronto, of African/Caribbean descent, she is the author of *40 Dayz* and *Motion In Poetry*, and the acclaimed play *Aneemah's Spot*. *Page 151*

Teeanna Munro (maternal last names: Philips, King, and Taylor), a spoken word artist, is the proud Black daughter of strong enduring women and storytellers who journeyed to Northern Alberta from Oklahoma in 1911, eventually creating deep rhythmic roots in Vancouver 1929. *Page 181*

N Oji Mzilikazi is a Canadian by way of Trinidad. He is a columnist for the *Montreal Community Contact*, is published in *Beyond Sangre Grande: Caribbean Writing Today*, and has two books scheduled for release in 2013. He blogs at *nojimzilikazi.com*. *Page 82*

Komi Olafimihan a.k.a. Poetic Speed is an artist from Kaduna, Nigeria. He is a member of the 2009 Canadian Festival of Spoken Word Slam championship team, The Recipe. He has authored *Improvisation in Architecture*, a critical study of the Makoko fishing community of Lagos. *Page 168*

Oni the Haitian Sensation, Godmother of Canadian Slam, Chalmers Award winning, Boxer, Politician, Academic, Polyglot, Mom, author of *Ghettostocracy*, directed Canada's first National Spoken Word festival, *the Canadian Spoken Wordlympics*. Haitian, Cuban, Chinese, Arawak, PanAfrican, European Hybrid, made in Canada. *Pages 204, 205*

Ikenna (OpenSecret) Onyegbula was born in Nigeria and raised on three different continents. He is a member of two different Canadian National poetry slam championship teams, while representing Ottawa. He is also the 2011 Canadian Individual Slam champion. *Page 210*

M. NourbeSe Philip is a poet, essayist, novelist and playwright who lives in the space-time of Toronto. Among her best known works are *She Tries Her Tongue, Looking for Livingstone,* and *Harriet's Daughter.* Her most recent work is *Zong! Page 37*

Queenie: Award winning author, performance poet Queenie a.k.a. Valerie Mason-John is an Albertan residing in BC. She is of slave stock from Sierra Leone, and born in Britain. It's possible she is related to the McCarthys of Nova Scotia. *Page 96*

Bercham Richards a.k.a. Dirt Gritie is an Edmonton, Alberta born Hip-Hop Artist/Spoken Word Poet of Jamaican/Vincentian heritage. Co-Founder of Music for Mavericks & Breath in Poetry Collective, and member of Politic Live, his latest album, *Ellipsis,* was released June 2012. *Page 237*

Joy Russell, born in Belize, came to Canada in the sixties. Her work includes the PodPlay *Days of Old*, and poetry, which has appeared in numerous publications such as *The Best Canadian Poetry in English 2008*. She lives in B.C. *Page 75*

Wayne Salmon, writer, photographer, born in Kingston, Jamaica, currently resides in Toronto, Canada. Published in *Flava*, he is at work on a collection of poems and a book of carbon photographs documenting the festival formerly known as Caribana. *Page 85*

Seble Samuel is a Montreal-based writer with Ethiopian roots. Her family immigrated to Canada in the 1980s. *Page 90*

Scruffmouth is a Canadian-Jamaican spoken poet, performer and scribe with the ability to condense issues of social justice, knowledge of self, identity, philosophy, history and freedom into creative poems for the page and the stage. *Page 155*

Jason "Blackbird" Selman, Montreal-born poet and musician (trumpet) is author of *The Freedom I Stole* and co-editor of *Talking Book* which chronicles the work of the Kalm Unity Vibe Collective of which he is a member. He is of Barbadian parentage. *Page 157*

Olive Senior, born in Jamaica, has 3 poetry books: *Talking of Trees* (1985), *Gardening in the Tropics* (1994), and *Over the Roofs of the World* (2005). *Summer Lightning* (1986) won the Commonwealth Writers Prize for short fiction. Her first novel, *Dancing Lessons*, was shortlisted for the 2012 Commonwealth Book Prize, Canada region. *Pages 35, 36*

Prufrock Shadowrunner, poet, rapper, DJ, actor,was national spoken word champion, 2010 and Toronto international poetry slam champion, 2011. Ontario resident of Black Jamaican background, he was born in Canada in the 80s. He released his CD *R.I.P. Charlie* with missing linx, 2012. *Page 227*

Storma Sire, children's author/illustrator, was born in B.C. from descendents of slave escapees from the U.S., and is of Ghanaian ancestry.

Her novel *Lessons in Magic* won Best Emerging Author/Illustrator in Children's Literature from Canada Council, and she has illustrated for UBC. *Page 91*

Charles C. Smith, poet, essayist, and university lecturer, won second prize for his play *Last Days for the Desperate* from Black Theatre Canada. Author of *Partial Lives* and the chapbook *Fleurette Africaine*, 2012, he is currently working on a multidisciplinary performance piece. *Pages 71, 73*

Deanna (D-NA) Smith is a Bajan-rooted, Montreal-flowering poet enjoying her love affair with words as a speech-language pathologist and active member of the "Throw Poetry" and "Kalmunity Vibe" collectives. A follow up to her chapbook *Full Circle* is in development. *Page 170*

Titilope Sonuga is a Nigerian-born spoken word poet and winner of the 2011 CAA Emerging Writer Award for her first book, *Down To Earth*. She currently resides in Edmonton and is the founder of the Breath In Poetry Collective. *www.titilope.ca* *Page 161*

Anita Stewart, Jamaican-born performance artist, resides in Brampton, Ontario. Her work is published in *Dub Poetry – 19 Poets from England and Jamaica* and *Utterances and Incantations: Women, Poetry and Dub*, and recorded in *Woman Talk* and "word soun' 'ave powah" spoken word albums. *Page 135*

Blossom Thom started life in Guyana. She immigrated to Southern Ontario with her family, where she was raised and schooled. Her heart led her to Montreal, Quebec where she now makes her home. Blossom's poetry appeared online in *BareBack Magazine*. *Page 92*

Andrea Thompson is a writer, performer and pioneer of the Canadian Spoken Word scene. She is the co-editor of *Other Tongues: Mixed Race Women Speak Out*, and currently teaches Spoken Word through the Ontario College of Art and Design. *Page 49*

Zakiya Toby was born, raised and currently resides in Ontario. She is a first-generation Canadian with Trinidadian lineage. She is the author of *From My Heart To Yours*, available on Amazon.com. *Page 98*

Frederick Ward: Born: Kansas City, 1937; attended Lincoln High School, University of Missouri, Kansas City Conservatory of Music, Advanced School of Contemporary Music (Toronto); taught at Dalhousie University, Dawson College; published *Riverlisp* (1974), *Nobody Called Me Mine* (1977), *A Room Full of Balloons* (1981). *Page 48*

Sharon Welch is a first-generation Canadian born in Toronto, but raised in Hamilton, Ontario where she currently resides. She's the daughter of Jamaican-born parents and is currently working on her first book. *Page 240*

Marlon "Arlo Maverick" Wilson is an Alberta-based poet and hip-hop MC with 3X WCMA-nominated hip-hop group Politic Live. Of Jamaican heritage, Wilson is a first generation Canadian hoping to create a legacy that demonstrates art's ability to create social change. *Page 234*

Brandon Wint is a Toronto-born, Ottawa-based writer, performer and teacher, of Jamaican and Bajan parentage. He is a two time Canadian champion of slam poetry and the co-author of *September*, his most recent chapbook (with Ikenna Onyegbula). *Page 219*

David Woods is a poet, playwright and visual artist from Dartmouth, N.S. Author of *Native Song* (1990), and *Native Song Revised* (2008), he won the Nova Scotia Poetry Award (1989), National Black Poetry Competition Prize (1999), and the George Elliott Clarke Literary Award (1998, 1999). *Page 34*

adrian "gryphen" worrell is an educator, artist-philosopher and semi-professional troll based in scarborough, ontario. in early 2013 he released a spoken word ep "scenes from a winter home" and "neotony" a book of poems. contact: *a.k.worrell@facebook.com Page 61*

Akhaji Zakiya, an award-winning poet, is expanding her writing repertoire to include short stories and novellas about women loving. A born and raised Torontonian, Akhaji's roots extend from West Africa to Barbados. Check out her recent work at *akhajizakiya.com Page188*

The Editors

Valerie Mason-John, a.k.a Queenie, grew up in orphanages and foster homes, and at age 14 was living on the streets of London. This start in life has been the inspiration for much of her work. She has received several awards for her contribution to the African and Asian diaspora, including an honorary Doctorate of Letters from a British university for her lifetime achievements. Her first novel, a fictional memoir titled *Borrowed Body,* won the Mind Book of the Year Award in 2006. She has just completed her second novel, unpublished, *The War Done Done,* which brings North America, the U.K. and blood diamonds from Sierra Leone together to tell a poignant family saga. She is also co-writing a book exploring a Buddhist approach to recovery from addictions and compulsive behaviours. Mason-John is also currently touring her one-woman show *Brown Girl In The Ring,* a poetic monologue and a regal meditation on racism. She was the coach of the winning Slam team, *Breath in Poetry* (Edmonton) at the Canadian festival of Spoken Word, 2011. Mason-John works as a Bully doctor, a life coach and master trainer in the field of anti-bullying, conflict transformation, restorative justice, addictions and leadership skills. For more information about her one-woman show or work:

bullydoctor@gmail.com; *www.valeriemason-john.com*; *www.bullyvictimbystander.com*; *www.facebook.com/IntoBEingLifeCoachingServices*

Kevan Anthony Cameron, also known as Scruffmouth, is a poet, performer and scribe. He was born in Edmonton, Alberta to Jamaican parents and now lives in Burnaby, B.C. where he works as a performer, facilitator and coach. His poetic style is a blend of spoken dub poetry, lyrical wordplay, and storytelling. Kevan is a graduate of Simon Fraser University, where he played men's varsity soccer and received his bachelor's degree in General Studies with a focus on liberal arts, philosophy and history. After playing soccer at the collegiate, international and professional levels, a debilitating injury on the pitch forced Mr. Cameron to use his voice and step up to the performance poetry stage. He is a veteran of poetry slam in North America, and has performed and featured at local venues and spoken word festivals in the Canada, the U.S. and worldwide. He has studied West African music, dance, history and culture and continues to innovate new forms of creative expression through his poetry and writing. Scruffmouth is a full member of the Alliance of Canadian Cinema, Television and Radio Artists as well as the Union of B.C. Performers. He is creative director for Black Dot Roots and Culture Collective, *www.blackdotcollective.org*—a community group focused on educational, creative and celebratory programming to connect the dots and envision the big picture.

He can be reached at *scruffmouth@gmail.com* or *@Scruffmouth*.